DATE DUE

JE 20 '89			
AR 1 '99			
MY 19 00			

Modern Critical Interpretations

E. M. Forster's
A Passage to India

Modern Critical Interpretations

These and other titles in preparation

Modern Critical Interpretations

E. M. Forster's
A Passage to India

Edited and with an introduction by

Harold Bloom
Sterling Professor of the Humanities
Yale University

Chelsea House Publishers ◇ 1987
NEW YORK ◇ NEW HAVEN ◇ PHILADELPHIA

© 1987 by Chelsea House Publishers, a division
of Chelsea House Educational Communications, Inc.,
    95 Madison Avenue, New York, NY 10016
    345 Whitney Avenue, New Haven, CT 06511
    5014 West Chester Pike, Edgemont, PA 19028

Introduction © 1987 by Harold Bloom

Printed and bound in the United States of America

∞ The paper used in this publication meets the minimum
requirements of the American National Standard for
Permanence of Paper for Printed Library Materials,
Z39.48–1984.

Library of Congress Cataloging-in-Publication Data
E. M. Forster's A passage to India.
    (Modern critical interpretations)
    Bibliography: p.
    Includes index.
    1. Forster, E. M. (Edward Morgan), 1879–1970.
Passage to India.   I. Bloom, Harold.   II. Series.
PR6011.058P3717   1987   823'.912   86–18850
ISBN 1–55546–018–6

Contents

Editor's Note

This book brings together what I consider to be the best criticism available of E. M. Forster's novel *A Passage to India*, arranged in the chronological order of its original publication. I am grateful to Jennifer Wagner for her aid in editing this volume.

My introduction ponders the complexities of the novel's singular religious stance, relating it to Forster's *Alexandria: A History and a Guide* and *The Hill of Devi*. Lionel Trilling inevitably begins the chronological sequence with his generous appreciation of Forster's liberal imagination at work in the novel. Very close to Trilling's emphasis is that of Malcolm Bradbury, whose Forster is both Victorian and modern, an appealer to and for values, and yet as dark as Melville in his cosmological implications.

K. Natwar-Singh, in a personal tribute to Forster, finds parallels between Forster and Nehru in their views as to the failure of the English and the Indians truly to understand one another. Expounding the dialectics of language and silence in *A Passage to India*, Michael Orange ascribes the book's aesthetic success to the stylistic delicacy that informs its heightened rhetorical self-consciousness.

A very intricate analysis of the novel by Barbara Rosecrance concludes with the persuasive judgment that the book's ordered language, its detachment and coherence, at once make it near perfect, and yet an impasse for Forster himself.

Rustom Bharucha, finding Forster's personal friendships reflected in the relationship between Fielding and Aziz, intimates that the India of the novel is represented by the same mode through which Forster depicted his own friendships. In the final essay, printed here for the first time, Sara Suleri subtly uncovers in Forster an erotic will-to-power over India, a will that makes of Adela Quested "a conduit or a passageway for the aborted eroticism between the European Fielding and the Indian Aziz."

Introduction

I

E. M. Forster's canonical critic was Lionel Trilling, who might have written Forster's novels had Forster not written them and had Trilling been English. Trilling ended his book on Forster (1924) with the tribute that forever exalts the author of *Howards End* and *A Passage to India* as one of those storytellers whose efforts "work without man's consciousness of them, and even against his conscious will." In Trilling's sympathetic interpretation (or identification), Forster was the true antithesis to the world of telegrams and anger:

> A world at war is necessarily a world of will; in a world at war
> Forster reminds us of a world where the will is not everything,
> of a world of true order, of the necessary connection of passion
> and prose, and of the strange paradoxes of being human. He is
> one of those who raise the shield of Achilles, which is the moral
> intelligence of art, against the panic and emptiness which make
> their onset when the will is tired from its own excess.

Trilling subtly echoed Forster's own response to World War I, a response which Forster recalled as an immersion in Blake, William Morris, the early T. S. Eliot, J. K. Huysmans, Yeats: "They took me into a country where the will was not everything." Yet one can wonder whether Forster and Trilling, prophets of the liberal imagination, did not yield to a vision where there was not quite enough conscious will. *A Passage to India*, Forster's most famous work, can sustain many rereadings, so intricate is its orchestration. It is one of only a few novels of this century that is *written-through*, in the musical sense of thorough composition. But reading it yet again, after twenty years away from it, I find it to be a narrative all of whose principal figures —Aziz, Fielding, Adela Quested, Mrs. Moore, Godbole—lack conscious will. Doubtless, this is Forster's deliberate art,

1

but the consequence is curious; the characters do not sustain rereading so well as the novel does, because none is larger than the book. Poldy holds my imagination quite apart from Joyce's *Ulysses,* as Isabel Archer does in James's *The Portrait of a Lady,* or indeed as Mrs. Wilcox does in Forster's *Howards End,* at least while she is represented as being alive. The aesthetic puzzle of *A Passage to India* is why Aziz and Fielding could not have been stronger and more vivid beings than they are.

What matters most in *A Passage to India* is India, and not any Indians nor any English. But this assertion requires amendment, since Forster's India is not so much a social or cultural reality as it is an enigmatic vision of the Hindu religion, or rather of the Hindu religion as it is reimagined by the English liberal mind at its most sensitive and scrupulous. The largest surprise of a careful rereading of *A Passage to India* after so many years is that, in some aspects, it now seems a strikingly *religious* book. Forster shows us what we never ought to have forgotten, which is that any distinction between religious and secular literature is finally a mere political or societal polemic, but is neither a spiritual nor an aesthetic judgment. There is no sacred literature and no post-sacred literature, great or good. *A Passage to India* falls perhaps just short of greatness, in a strict aesthetic judgment, but spiritually it is an extraordinary achievement.

T. S. Eliot consciously strove to be a devotional poet, and certainly did become a Christian polemicist as a cultural and literary critic. Forster, an amiable freethinker and secular humanist, in his *Commonplace Book* admirably compared himself to Eliot:

> With Eliot? I feel now to be as far ahead of him as I was once behind. Always a distance—and a respectful one. How I dislike his homage to pain! What a mind except the human could have excogitated it? Of course there's pain on and off through each individual's life, and pain at the end of most lives. You can't shirk it and so on. But why should it be endorsed by the school-master and sanctified by the priest until
>
> > the fire and the rose are one
>
> when so much of it is caused by disease or by bullies? It is here that Eliot becomes unsatisfactory as a seer.

One could add: it is here that Forster becomes most satisfactory as a seer, for that is the peculiar excellence of *A Passage to India*. We are reminded that Forster is another of John Ruskin's heirs, together with Proust, whom Forster rightly admired above all other modern novelists. Forster too wishes *to make us see,* in the hope that by seeing we will learn to connect, with ourselves and with others, and like Ruskin, Forster knows that seeing in this strong sense is religious, but in a mode beyond dogmatism.

II

A Passage to India, published in 1924, reflects Forster's service as private secretary to the Maharajah of Dewas State Senior in 1921–22, which in turn issued from his Indian visit of 1912–13 with G. Lowes Dickinson. It was not until 1953 that Forster published *The Hill of Devi,* utilizing letters he had written home from India, both forty and thirty years before. *The Hill of Devi* celebrates Forster's Maharajah as a kind of saint, indeed as a religious genius, though Forster is anything but persuasive when he attempts to sustain his judgment of his friend and employer. What does come through is Forster's appreciation of certain elements in Hinduism, an appreciation that achieves its apotheosis in *A Passage to India,* and particularly in "Temple," the novel's foreshortened final part. Forster's ultimate tribute to his Maharajah, a muddler in practical matters and so one who died in disgrace, is a singular testimony for a freethinker. *The Hill of Devi* concludes with what must be called a mystical apprehension:

> His religion was the deepest thing in him. It ought to be studied—neither by the psychologist nor by the mythologist but by the individual who has experienced similar promptings. He penetrated into rare regions and he was always hoping that others would follow him there.

What are those promptings? Where are those regions? Are these the questions fleshed out by *A Passage to India?* After observing the mystical Maharajah dance before the altar of the God Krishna, Forster quotes from a letter by the Maharajah describing the festival, and then attempts what replies seem possible:

> Such was his account. But what did he feel when he danced like King David before the altar? What were his religious opinions?
>   The first question is easier to answer than the second. He felt as King David and other mystics have felt when they are in the mystic state. He presented well-known characteristics. He was convinced that he was in touch with the reality he called Krishna. And he was unconscious of the world around him. "You can come in during my observances tomorrow and see me if you

like, but I shall not know that you are there," he once told Malcolm. And he didn't know. He was in an abnormal but recognisable state; psychologists have studied it.

More interesting, and more elusive, are his religious opinions. The unseen was always close to him, even when he was joking or intriguing. Red paint on a stone could evoke it. Like most people, he implied beliefs and formulated rules for behaviour, and since he had a lively mind, he was often inconsistent. It was difficult to be sure what he did believe (outside the great mystic moments) or what he thought right or wrong. Indians are even more puzzling than Westerners here. Mr. Shastri, a spiritual and subtle Brahmin, once uttered a puzzler: "If the Gods do a thing, it is a reason for men not to do it." No doubt he was in a particular religious mood. In another mood he would have urged us to imitate the Gods. And the Maharajah was all moods. They played over his face, they agitated his delicate feet and hands. To get any pronouncement from so mercurial a creature on the subject, say, of asceticism, was impossible. As a boy, he had thought of retiring from the world, and it was an ideal which he cherished throughout his life, and which, at the end, he would have done well to practise. Yet he would condemn asceticism, declare that salvation could not be reached through it, that it might be Vedantic but it was not Vedic, and matter and spirit must both be given their due. Nothing too much! In such a mood he seemed Greek.

He believed in the heart, and here we reach firmer ground. "I stand for the heart. To the dogs with the head," cries Herman Melville, and he would have agreed. Affection, or the possibility of it, quivered through everything, from Gokul Ashtami down to daily human relationships. When I returned to England and he heard that I was worried because the post-war world of the '20's would not add up into sense, he sent me a message. "Tell him," it ran, "tell him from me to follow his heart, and his mind will see everything clear." The message as phrased is too facile: doors open into silliness at once. But to remember and respect and prefer the heart, to have the instinct which follows it wherever possible—what surer help than that could one have through life? What better hope of clarification? Melville goes on: "The reason that the mass of men fear God and at bottom dislike Him, is because they rather distrust His heart." With that too he would have agreed.

With all respect for Forster, neither he nor his prince is coherent here, and I suspect that Forster is weakly misreading Melville, who is both more ironic and more Gnostic than Forster chooses to realize. Melville, too, distrusts the heart of Jehovah, and consigns the head to the dogs precisely because he associates the head with Jehovah and identifies Jehovah with the Demiurge, the god of this world. More vital would be the question: what does Professor Godbole in *A Passage to India* believe? Is he more coherent than the Maharajah, and does Forster himself achieve a more unified vision there than he does in *The Hill of Devi*?

Criticism from Lionel Trilling on has evaded these questions, but such evasion is inevitable because Forster may be vulnerable to the indictment that he himself made against Joseph Conrad, to the effect that

> he is misty in the middle as well as at the edges, that the secret casket of his genius contains a vapour rather than a jewel; and that we need not try to write him down philosophically, because there is, in this particular direction, nothing to write. No creed, in fact. Only opinions, and the right to throw them overboard when facts make them look absurd. Opinions held under the semblance of eternity, girt with the sea, crowned with the stars, and therefore easily mistaken for a creed.

Heart of Darkness sustains Forster's gentle wit, but *Nostromo* does not. Is there a vapor rather than a jewel in Forster's consciousness of Hinduism, at least as represented in *A Passage to India?* "Hinduism" may be the wrong word in that question; "religion" would be better, and "spirituality" better yet. For I do not read Forster as being either hungry for belief or skeptical of it. Rather, he seems to me an Alexandrian, of the third century before the common era, an age celebrated in his *Alexandria: A History and a Guide* (1922), a book that goes back to his happy years in Alexandria (1915–19). In some curious sense, Forster's India is Alexandrian, and his vision of Hinduism is Plotinean. *A Passage to India* is a narrative of Neo-Platonic spirituality, and the true heroine of that narrative, Mrs. Moore, is the Alexandrian figure of Wisdom, the Sophia, as set forth in the Hellenistic Jewish Wisdom of Solomon. Of Wisdom, or Sophia, Forster says: "She is a messenger who bridges the gulf and makes us friends of God," which is a useful description of the narrative function of Mrs. Moore. And after quoting Plotinus (in a passage that includes one of his book's epigraphs): "To any vision must be brought an eye adapted to what is to be seen," Forster comments:

> This sublime passage suggests three comments, with which our glance at Plotinus must close. In the first place its tone is reli-

gious, and in this it is typical of all Alexandrian philosophy. In the second place it lays stress on behaviour and training; the Supreme Vision cannot be acquired by magic tricks—only those will see it who are fit to see. And in the third place the vision of oneself and the vision of God are really the same, because each individual *is* God, if only he knew it. And here is the great difference between Plotinus and Christianity. The Christian promise is that a man shall see God, the Neo-Platonic—like the Indian—that he shall be God. Perhaps, on the quays of Alexandria, Plotinus talked with Hindu merchants who came to the town. At all events his system can be paralleled in the religious writings of India. He comes nearer than any other Greek philosopher to the thought of the East.

Forster's Alexandria is in the first place personal; he associated the city always with his sexual maturation as a homosexual. But, as the book *Alexandria* shrewdly shows, Forster finds his precursor culture in ancient Alexandria; indeed he helps to teach us that we are all Alexandrians, insofar as we now live in a literary culture. Forster's insight is massively supported by the historian F. E. Peters in the great study *The Harvest of Hellenism,* when he catalogs our debts to the Eastern Hellenism of Alexandria:

> Its monuments are gnosticism, the university, the catechetical school, pastoral poetry, monasticism, the romance, grammar, lexicography, city planning, theology, canon law, heresy, and scholasticism.

Forster would have added, thinking of the Ptolemaic Alexandria of 331–30 B.C.E., that the most relevant legacy was an eclectic and tolerant liberal humanism, scientific and scholarly, exalting the values of affection over those of belief. That is already the vision of *A Passage to India,* and it opens to the novel's central spiritual question: how are the divine and the human linked? In *Alexandria,* Forster presents us with a clue by his account of the Arian heresy:

> Christ is the Son of God. Then is he not younger than God? Arius held that he was and that there was a period before time began when the First Person of the Trinity existed and the Second did not. A typical Alexandrian theologian, occupied with the favourite problem of linking human and divine, Arius thought to solve the problem by making the link predominately human. He did not deny the Godhead of Christ, but he did make him

inferior to the Father—of *like* substance, not of the *same* substance, which was the view held by Athanasius, and stamped as orthodox by the Council of Nicaea. Moreover the Arian Christ, like the Gnostic Demiurge, made the world;—creation, an inferior activity, being entrusted to him by the Father, who had Himself created nothing but Christ.

It is easy to see why Arianism became popular. By making Christ younger and lower than God it brought him nearer to us—indeed it tended to level him into a mere good man and to forestall Unitarianism. It appealed to the untheologically minded, to emperors and even more to empresses. But St. Athanasius, who viewed the innovation with an expert eye, saw that while it popularised Christ it isolated God, and he fought it with vigour and venom. His success has been described. It was condemned as heretical in 325, and by the end of the century had been expelled from orthodox Christendom. Of the theatre of this ancient strife no trace remains at Alexandria; the church of St. Mark where Arius was presbyter has vanished: so have the churches where Athanasius thundered—St. Theonas and the Caesareum. Nor do we know in which street Arius died of epilepsy. But the strife still continues in the hearts of men, who always tend to magnify the human in the divine, and it is probable that many an individual Christian to-day is an Arian without knowing it.

To magnify the human in the divine is certainly Forster's quest, and appears to be his interpretation of Hinduism in *A Passage to India*:

> Down in the sacred corridors, joy had seethed to jollity. It was their duty to play various games to amuse the newly born God, and to simulate his sports with the wanton dairymaids of Brindaban. Butter played a prominent part in these. When the cradle had been removed, the principal nobles of the state gathered together for an innocent frolic. They removed their turbans, and one put a lump of butter on his forehead, and waited for it to slide down his nose into his mouth. Before it could arrive, another stole up behind him, snatched the melting morsel, and swallowed it himself. All laughed exultantly at discovering that the divine sense of humour coincided with their own. "God si love!" There is fun in heaven. God can play practical jokes upon Himself, draw chairs away from beneath His own posteriors,

set His own turbans on fire, and steal His own petticoats when
He bathes. By sacrificing good taste, this worship achieved what
Christianity has shirked: the inclusion of merriment. All spirit
as well as all matter must participate in salvation, and if practical
jokes are banned, the circle is incomplete. Having swallowed
the butter, they played another game which chanced to be graceful: the fondling of Shri Krishna under the similitude of a child.
A pretty red and gold ball is thrown, and he who catches it
chooses a child from the crowd, raises it in his arms, and carries
it round to be caressed. All stroke the darling creature for the
Creator's sake, and murmur happy words. The child is restored
to his parents, the ball thrown on, and another child becomes
for a moment the World's desire. And the Lord bounds hither
and thither through the aisles, chance, and the sport of chance,
irradiating little mortals with His immortality. . . . When they
had played this long enough—and being exempt from boredom,
they played it again and again, they played it again and again—
they took many sticks and hit them together, whack smack, as
though they fought the Pandava wars, and threshed and churned
with them, and later on they hung from the roof of the temple,
in a net, a great black earthenware jar, which was painted here
and there with red, and wreathed with dried figs. Now came a
rousing sport. Springing up, they struck at the jar with their
sticks. It cracked, broke, and a mass of greasy rice and milk
poured on to their faces. They ate and smeared one another's
mouths and dived between each other's legs for what had been
pashed upon the carpet. This way and that spread the divine
mess, until the line of schoolboys, who had somewhat fended
off the crowd, broke for their share. The corridors, the court-
yard, were filled with benign confusion. Also the flies awoke
and claimed their share of God's bounty. There was no quar-
relling, owing to the nature of the gift, for blessed is the man
who confers it on another, he imitates God. And those "imi-
tations," those "substitutions," continued to flicker through the
assembly for many hours, awaking in each man, according to
his capacity, an emotion that he would not have had otherwise.
No definite image survived; at the Birth it was questionable
whether a silver doll or a mud village, or a silk napkin, or an
intangible spirit, or a pious resolution, had been born. Perhaps
all these things! Perhaps none! Perhaps all birth is an allegory!

Still, it was the main event of the religious year. It caused strange thoughts. Covered with grease and dust, Professor Godbole had once more developed the life of his spirit. He had, with increasing vividness, again seen Mrs. Moore, and round her faintly clinging forms of trouble. He was a Brahman, she Christian, but it made no difference, it made no difference whether she was a trick of his memory or a telepathic appeal. It was his duty, as it was his desire, to place himself in the position of the God and to love her, and to place himself in her position and to say to the God, "Come, come, come, come." This was all he could do. How inadequate! But each according to his own capacities, and he knew that his own were small. "One old Englishwoman and one little, little wasp," he thought, as he stepped out of the temple into the grey of a pouring wet morning. "It does not seem much, still it is more than I am myself."

Professor Godbole's epiphany, his linkage of Mrs. Moore's receptivity toward the wasp with his own receptivity toward Mrs. Moore, has been much admired by critics, deservedly so. In this moment-of-moments, Godbole receives Mrs. Moore into Forster's own faithless faith: a religion of love between equals, as opposed to Christianity, a religion of love between the incommensurate Jehovah and his creatures. But though beautifully executed, Forster's vision of Godbole and Mrs. Moore is spiritually a little too easy. Forster knew that, and the finest moment in *A Passage to India* encompasses this knowing. It comes in a sublime juxtaposition, in the crossing between the conclusion of part 2, "Caves," and the beginning of part 3, "Temple," where Godbole is seen standing in the presence of God. The brief and beautiful chapter 32 that concludes "Caves" returns Fielding to a Western and Ruskinian vision of form in Venice:

Egypt was charming—a green strip of carpet and walking up and down it four sorts of animals and one sort of man. Fielding's business took him there for a few days. He re-embarked at Alexandria—bright blue sky, constant wind, clean low coastline, as against the intricacies of Bombay. Crete welcomed him next with the long snowy ridge of its mountains, and then came Venice. As he landed on the piazzetta a cup of beauty was lifted to his lips, and he drank with a sense of disloyalty. The buildings of Venice, like the mountains of Crete and the fields of Egypt, stood in the right place, whereas in poor India everything was placed wrong. He had forgotten the beauty of form among idol temples and lumpy hills; indeed, without form, how can there be beauty? Form stammered here and there in a mosque, became rigid through nervousness even, but oh these Italian churches! San Giorgio standing on the island which could scarcely have risen from the waves without it, the Salute holding the entrance of a canal which, but for it, would not be the Grand Canal! In the old undergraduate days he had wrapped himself up in the many-coloured blanket of St. Mark's, but something more precious than mosaics and marbles was offered to him now: the harmony between the works of man and the earth that upholds them, the civilization that has escaped muddle, the spirit in a reasonable form, with flesh and blood subsisting. Writing picture post-cards to his Indian friends, he felt that all of them would miss the joys he experienced now, the joys of form, and that this constituted a serious barrier. They would see the sumptuousness of Venice, not its shape, and though Venice was not Europe, it was part of the Mediterranean harmony. The Mediterranean is the human norm. When men leave that exquisite lake, whether through the Bosphorus or the Pillars of Hercules, they approach the monstrous and extraordinary; and the southern exit leads to the strangest experience of all. Turning his back on it yet again, he took the train northward, and tender romantic fancies that he thought were dead for ever, flowered when he saw the buttercups and daisies of June.

After the muddle of India, where "everything was placed wrong," Fielding learns again "the beauty of form." Alexandria, like Venice, is part of the Mediterranean harmony, the human norm, but India is the cosmos of "the monstrous and extraordinary." Fielding confronting the Venetian churches has absolutely nothing in common with Professor Godbole confronting the God Krishna at the opposite end of the same strip of carpet upon which Godbole stands. Forster is too wise not to know that the passage to India is only a passage. A passage is a journey, or an occurrence between two persons. Fielding and Aziz do not quite make the passage together, do not exchange vows that bind. Perhaps that recognition of limits is the ultimate beauty of form in *A Passage to India*.

A Passage to India

Lionel Trilling

The years between 1910 and 1914 were the vestibule to what Forster has called "the sinister corridor of our age." *Howards End* records the sense of Germany's growing strength; Mr. Schlegel, father of Helen and Margaret, had voluntarily exiled himself from the old Germany of philosophers, musicians and little courts and he spoke bitterly of the new imperialism to which "money [was] supremely useful; intellect, rather useful; imagination, of no use at all."

Not many books of the time were so precisely sensitive to the situation, yet a kind of sultry premonitory hush comes over literature in these years. The hope of the first decade of the century has been checked. The athletic quality of intelligence which seemed to mark the work of even five years earlier has subsided.

In 1910, following the publication of *Howards End,* Forster projected two novels but wrote neither. The next year he finished a play, *The Heart of Bosnia,* which, by his own account, was not good, and which has never been produced or published. In 1912, Forster, in company with Dickinson and R. C. Trevelyan, sailed for India. Dickinson, travelling on one of the fellowships established by Albert Kahn in the interests of international understanding, had official visits and tours to make and the friends separated at Bombay. But their itineraries crossed several times and they spent a fortnight as guests of the Maharajah of Chhatarpur who loved Dickinson and philosophy—"Tell me, Mr. Dickinson, where is God?" the Maharajah

From *E. M. Forster: A Study by Lionel Trilling.* © 1944 by Lionel Trilling. Hogarth Press, 1951.

said. "Can Herbert Spencer lead me to him, or should I prefer George Henry Lewes? Oh when will Krishna come and be my friend? Oh Mr. Dickinson!"

The two travellers came away from India with widely different feelings. Dickinson, who was to love China, was not comfortable in India. Displeased as he was by her British rulers, he was not pleased with India itself. "There is no solution to the problem of governing India," he wrote. "Our presence is a curse both to them and to us. Our going away will be worse. I believe that to the last word. And *why* can't the races meet? Simply because the Indians *bore* the English. That is the simple adamantine fact." It is not an enlightening or even a serious view of the situation, and Forster, dissenting from it, speaks of the "peace and happiness" which he himself found in India in 1912 and again on his second visit ten years later.

The best fruit of the Indian journey was to be *A Passage to India,* but meanwhile Forster wrote several short pieces on Indian life of which two, "The Suppliant" and "Advance, India!" (both reprinted in *Abinger Harvest*) admirably depict the comic, sad confusion of a nation torn between two cultures.

He began to sketch the Indian novel, but the war postponed its completion for a decade. And the war quite destroyed the project for a critical study of Samuel Butler, with whose mind Forster's has community at so many points. But the war, which sent Forster to non-combatant service in Egypt, developed in him the interest in Imperial conduct and policy which the Indian tour had begun. Hitherto Forster's political concern had been intense but perhaps abstract; now it became increasingly immediate. The three Egyptian years gave him not only the material for two books and many essays, but also a firm position on the Imperial question.

The first of Forster's Egyptian books is the guidebook, *Alexandria: A History and a Guide;* its introductory account of the city's history gives Forster the opportunity to display his love of the Hellenic and naturalistic, his contempt for the Christian and theological; its second part arranges tours to points of interest, and the whole job is scholarly, attractive and efficient. Much less can be said for *Pharos and Pharillon,* another venture into Alexandrian history and local colour. The volume is infused with the archness which has been noted earlier as the fault of Forster's first historical essays; the years have but intensified it. Under Forster's implacable gentleness, the past becomes what it should never be, quaint, harmless and ridiculous. Menelaos, Alexander, the Ptolemies, the Jews, the Arabs, the Christian theologians, the very lighthouse itself, all become submerged in high irony. This desperately persistent fault of taste is all the more surprising because Forster has himself so rightly characterized it in one of his best essays, "The Consolations of History."

> It is pleasant to be transferred from an office where one is afraid of a sergeant-major into an office where one can intimidate generals, and perhaps that is why History is so attractive to the more timid among us. We can recover self-confidence by snubbing the dead: . . . Tight little faces from Oxford, fish-shaped faces from Cambridge,—we cannot help having our dreams.

The same fault of lofty whimsicality inheres in other of the sketches which in *Abinger Harvest* are collected under the rubric of "The Past." Sufficiently objectionable in "Captain Edward Gibbon" and in "Voltaire's Laboratory," it becomes really bad in "Trooper Silas Tompkyns Comberbacke" and in "The Abbeys' Difficulties," the first of which dramatically reveals the open secret that the Trooper's real name was Samuel Taylor Coleridge, the second that the young people with whom the Abbeys had difficulty were Fanny and John Keats.

A single sentence of *Pharos and Pharillon* points away from this slim, feasting antiquarianism; speaking of Fort Kait Bey, Forster mentions the holes in it "made by Admiral Seymour when he bombarded the Fort in 1882 and laid the basis of our intercourse with modern Egypt." In 1920 Forster wrote his note for *The Government of Egypt,* a pamphlet of the International Section of the Labour Research Department, a Fabian organization. Although it does little save support the Committee's recommendation that Egypt be given either dominion status or autonomy and although it is scarcely interesting in itself, it indicates Forster's increasing interest in public affairs.

It was an angry interest. In 1934 Forster was to publish his biography of Dickinson, who had died two years before. Perhaps because Dickinson's life lacked tension or tone, perhaps because Forster wrote under some reserve, the biography is not a work of high distinction, but it serves to suggest the political atmosphere in which Forster lived. The crown of Dickinson's political life was his fight against what he called International Anarchy; his weapon, soon taken from his hands, was the League of Nations. He hoped to raise the minds of men above "the fighting attitude" of practical politics, but he could never, he confessed, formulate clearly "the great problem of the relation of ideals to passion and interest." This is, of course, Forster's own insistent question, but Forster's is an angrier mind than Dickinson's and any uncertainty he feels about the ultimate problems of politics does not prevent him from speaking out on matters of the moment.

England after the war was tense with class antagonism. In 1920 Forster became for a year the literary editor of the *Daily Herald,* a Labour paper to whose weekly literary page many well-known writers of liberal leanings contributed reviews. In the following years the amount of Forster's literary and political journalism, collected and uncollected, was considerable.

The political pieces are suffused with disillusionment about the war, a foreboding that a new war is imminent, a hatred of the stupidities of class rule. They pretend neither to originality of sentiment nor to practical perspicacity; they express, sometimes with anger, sometimes with bitterness, sometimes only with a kind of salutary irritation and disgust, the old emotions—the 19th century emotions, we almost feel, and we salute their directness—of a rational democrat confronting foolishness and pretence. Perhaps the most successful of these pieces is the essay "Me, Them and You." It is a review of the Sargent exhibition of 1925 in which, among all the aristocratic portraits, Sargent's pleasant, fanciful war picture, "Gassed," was hung. The situation was made for the satirist and Forster takes advantage of it in one of the truly successful pieces of modern invective.

> The portraits dominated. Gazing at each other over our heads, they said, "What would the country do without us? We have got the decorations and the pearls, we make fashions and wars, we have the largest houses and eat the best food, and control the most important industries, and breed the most valuable children, and ours is the Kingdom and the Power and the Glory." And, listening to their chorus, I felt this was so, and my clothes fitted worse and worse, and there seemed in all the universe no gulf wider than the gulf between Them and Me—no wider gulf, until I encountered You.
>
> You had been plentiful enough in the snow outside (your proper place) but I had not expected to find You here in the place of honour, too. Yours was by far the largest picture in the show. You were hung between Lady Cowdray and the Hon. Mrs. Langman, and You were entitled "Gassed." You were of godlike beauty—for the upper classes only allow the lower classes to appear in art on condition that they wash themselves and have classical features. These conditions you fulfilled. A line of golden-haired Apollos moved along a duck-board from left to right with bandages over their eyes. They had been blinded

by mustard gas. Others sat peacefully in the foreground, others approached through the middle distance. The battlefield was sad but tidy. No one complained, no one looked lousy or overtired, and the aeroplanes overhead struck the necessary note of the majesty of England. It was all that a great war picture should be, and it was modern because it managed to tell a new sort of lie. Many ladies and gentlemen fear that Romance is passing out of war with the sabres and the chargers. Sargent's masterpiece reassures them. He shows them that it is possible to suffer with a quiet grace under the new conditions, and Lady Cowdray and the Hon. Mrs. Langman, as they looked over the twenty feet of canvas that divided them, were able to say, "How touching," instead of "How obscene."

Less remarkable but filled with a fine irritation is the piece on the British Empire Exhibition at Wembley ("An Empire Is Born") and another on the Queen's Doll House ("The Doll Souse"). Forster's old antipathy to the clergy turns up again in political form in the verses which answer Bishop Welldon's public complaint of the profanity of the Labour Members of Parliament. One of the best of his essays, "My Wood," describes the growth of the property sense in himself after the purchase of a new tract of wood— "The other day I heard a twig snap in [my wood]. I was annoyed at first, for I thought that someone was blackberrying, and depreciating the value of the undergrowth. On coming nearer, I saw it was not a man who had trodden on the twig and snapped it, but a bird, and I felt pleased. My bird." The essay is especially to be noted because it states with almost startling explicitness a view of life which has been implicit in the novels:

> Our life on earth is, and ought to be, material and carnal. But we have not yet learned to manage our materialism and carnality properly; they are still entangled with the desire for ownership; where (in the words of Dante) "Possession is one with loss."

Over the anomalies of literary censorship Forster had long been exercised. In 1939 he was appointed by the Lord Chancellor to the Committee to examine the Law of Defamatory Libel. His 1935 address to the Paris *Congrès International des Ecrivains* on the subject of literary freedom constitutes a declaration of political faith.

> It seems to me that if nations keep on amassing armaments, they can no more help discharging their filth than an animal which keeps on eating can stop itself from excreting. This being so,

my job and the job of those who feel with me is an interim job. We have just to go on tinkering as well as we can with our old tools until the crash comes. When the crash comes, nothing is any good. After it—if there is an after—the task of civilization will be carried on by people whose training has been different from my own.

I am worried by thoughts of a war oftener than by thoughts of my own death, yet the line to be adopted over both these nuisances is the same. One must behave as if one is immortal, and as if civilization is eternal. Both statements are false—I shall not survive, no more will the great globe itself—both of them must be assumed to be true if we are to go on eating and working and travelling, and keep open a few breathing holes for the human spirit.

In 1922 Forster made a second journey to India and took up again the Indian story he had projected. *A Passage to India* appeared with great success in 1924.

A Passage to India is Forster's best known and most widely read novel. Public and political reasons no doubt account for this; in England the book was a matter for controversy and its success in America, as Forster himself explains it, was due to the superiority Americans could feel at the English botch of India. But the public, political nature of the book is not extraneous; it inheres in the novel's very shape and texture.

By many standards of criticism, this public, political quality works for good. *A Passage to India* is the most comfortable and even the most conventional of Forster's novels. It is under the control not only of the author's insight; a huge, hulking physical fact which he is not alone in seeing, requiring that the author submit to its veto-power. Consequently, this is the least surprising of Forster's novels, the least capricious and, indeed, the least personal. It quickly establishes the pattern for our emotions and keeps to it. We are at once taught to withhold our sympathies from the English officials, to give them to Mrs. Moore and to the "renegade" Fielding, to regard Adela Quested with remote interest and Aziz and his Indian friends with affectionate understanding.

Within this pattern we have, to be sure, all the quick, subtle modifications, the sudden strictness or relentings of judgment which are the best stuff of Forster's social imagination. But always the pattern remains public, simple and entirely easy to grasp. What distinguishes it from the patterns of similarly public and political novels is the rigor of its objectivity; it deals with unjust, hysterical emotion and it leads us, not to intense emotions about justice, but to cool poise and judgment—if we do not relent in our contempt for Ronny, we are at least forced to be aware that he is capable of noble, if stupid, feelings; the English girl who has the hallucination of an attempted rape by a native has engaged our sympathy by her rather dull decency; we are permitted no easy response to the benign Mrs. Moore, or to Fielding, who stands out against his own people, or to the native physician who is wrongly accused. This restraint of our emotions is an important element in the book's greatness.

With the public nature of the story goes a chastened and somewhat more public style than is usual with Forster, and a less arbitrary manner. Forster does not abandon his right to intrude into the novel, but his manner of intrusion is more circumspect than ever before. Perhaps this is because here, far less than in the English and Italian stories, he is in possession of truth; the Indian gods are not his gods, they are not genial and comprehensible. So far as the old Mediterranean deities of wise impulse and loving intelligence can go in India, Forster is at home; he thinks they can go far but not all the way, and a certain retraction of the intimacy of his style reflects his uncertainty. The acts of imagination by which Forster conveys the sense of the Indian gods are truly wonderful; they are, nevertheless, the acts of imagination not of a master of the truth but of an intelligent neophyte, still baffled.

So the public nature of the novel cannot be said to work wholly for good. For the first time Forster has put himself to the test of verisimilitude. Is this the truth about India? Is this the way the English act?—always? sometimes? never? Are Indians like this?—all of them? some of them? Why so many Moslems and so few Hindus? Why so much Hindu religion and so little Moslem? And then, finally, the disintegrating question, What is to be done?

Forster's gallery of English officials has of course been disputed in England; there have been many to say that the English are not like that. Even without knowledge we must suppose that the Indian Civil Service has its quota of decent, devoted and humble officials. But if Forster's portraits are perhaps angry exaggerations, anger can be illuminating—the English of Forster's Chandrapore are the limits toward which the English in India must approach, for Lord Acton was right, power does corrupt, absolute power does corrupt absolutely.

As for the representation of the Indians, that too can be judged here only on *a priori* grounds. Although the Indian are conceived in sympathy and affection, they are conceived with these emotions alone, and although all of them have charm, none of them has dignity; they touch our hearts but they never impress us. Once, at his vindication feast, Aziz is represented as "full of civilization . . . complete, dignified, rather hard" and for the first time Fielding treats him "with diffidence," but this only serves to remind us how lacking in dignity Aziz usually is. Very possibly this is the effect that Indians make upon even sensitive Westerners; Dickinson, as we have seen, was bored by them, and generations of subjection can diminish the habit of dignity and teach grown men the strategy of the little child.

These are not matters that we can settle; that they should have arisen at all is no doubt a fault of the novel. Quite apart from the fact that questions of verisimilitude diminish illusion, they indicate a certain inadequacy in the conception of the story. To represent the official English as so unremittingly bad and the Indians as so unremittingly feeble is to prevent the story from being sufficiently worked out in terms of the characters; the characters, that is, are *in* the events, the events are not in them: we want a larger Englishman than Fielding, a weightier Indian than Aziz.

These are faults, it is true, and Forster is the one novelist who could commit them and yet transcend and even put them to use. The relation of the characters to the events, for example, is the result of a severe imbalance in the relation of plot to story. Plot and story in this novel are not coextensive as they are in all Forster's other novels. The plot is precise, hard, crystallized and far simpler than any Forster has previously conceived. The story is beneath and above the plot and continues beyond it in time. It is, to be sure, created by the plot, it is the plot's manifold reverberation, but it is greater than the plot and contains it. The plot is as decisive as a judicial opinion; the story is an impulse, a tendency, a perception. The suspension of plot in the large circumambient sphere of story, the expansion of the story from the centre of plot, requires some of the subtlest manipulation that any novel has ever had. This relation of plot and story tells us that we are dealing with a political novel of an unusual kind. The characters are of sufficient size for the plot; they are not large enough for the story—and that indeed is the point of the story.

This, in outline, is the plot: Adela Quested arrives in India under the chaperonage of the elderly Mrs. Moore with whose son by a first marriage Adela has an "understanding." Both ladies are humane and Adela is liberal and they have an intense desire to "know India." This is a matter of some annoyance to Ronny, Mrs. Moore's son and Adela's fiancé, and of amused condescension to the dull people at the station who try to satisfy the ladies with elephant rides—only very *new* people try to *know* India. Both Mrs. Moore and Adela are chilled by Ronny; he has entirely adopted the point of view of the ruling race and has become a heavy-minded young judge with his dull dignity as his chief recognized asset. But despite Ronny's fussy certainty about what is and is not proper, Mrs. Moore steps into a mosque one evening and there makes the acquaintance of Aziz, a young Moslem doctor. Aziz is hurt and miserable, for he has just been snubbed; Mrs. Moore's kindness and simplicity soothe him. Between the two a friendship develops which politely includes Adela Quested. At last, by knowing Indians, the travellers will know India, and Aziz is even more delighted than they at the prospect of the relationship. To express his feelings he organizes a fantastically elaborate jaunt to the Marabar caves. Fielding, the principal of the local college, and Professor Godbole, a Hindu teacher, were also to have been of the party but they miss the train and Aziz goes ahead with the ladies and his absurd retinue. In one of the caves Mrs. Moore has a disturbing psychic experience and sends Aziz and Adela to continue the exploration without her. Adela, not a very attractive girl, has had her doubts about her engagement to Ronny, not a very attractive man, and now she ventures to speak of love to Aziz, quite abstractly but in a way both to offend him and disturb herself. In the cave the strap of her field-glasses is pulled and broken by someone in the darkness and she rushes out in a frenzy of hallucination that Aziz has attempted to rape her. The accusation makes the English of the station hysterical with noble rage. In every English mind there is the certainty that Aziz is guilty and the verdict is foregone. Only Fielding and Mrs. Moore do not share this certainty. Fielding, because of his liking for the young doctor, and Mrs. Moore, because of an intuition, are sure that the event could not have happened and that Adela is the victim of illusion. Fielding, who openly declares his partisanship, is ostracized, and Mrs. Moore, who only hints her opinion, is sent out of the country by her son; the journey in the terrible heat of the Indian May exhausts her and she dies on shipboard. At the trial Adela's illusion, fostered by the mass-hysteria of the English, becomes suddenly dispelled, she recants, Aziz is cleared, Fielding is vindicated and promoted, the Indians are happy, the English furious.

Thus the plot. And no doubt it is too much a plot of event, too easily open and shut. Nevertheless it is an admirable if obvious device for organizing an enormous amount of observation of both English and native society; it brings to spectacular virulence the latent antagonisms between rulers and ruled.

Of the Anglo-Indian society it is perhaps enough to say that, "more than it can hope to do in England," it lives by the beliefs of the English public school. It is arrogant, ignorant, insensitive—intelligent natives estimate that a year in India makes the pleasantest Englishman rude. And of all the English it is the women who insist most strongly on their superiority, who are the rawest and crudest in their manner. The men have a certain rough liking for the men of the subject race; for instance, Turton, Collector of the district, has "a contemptuous affection for the pawns he had moved about for so many years; they must be worth his pains." But the women, unchecked by any professional necessity or pride, think wholly in terms of the most elementary social prestige and Turton's wife lives for nothing else. "After all," Turton thinks but never dares say, "it's our women who make everything more difficult out here."

This is the result of the undeveloped heart. *A Passage to India* is not a radical novel; its data were gathered in 1912 and 1922, before the full spate of Indian nationalism; it is not concerned to show that the English should not be in India at all. Indeed, not until the end of the book is the question of the expulsion of the English mentioned, and the novel proceeds on an imperialistic premise—ironically, for it is not actually Forster's own—its chief point being that by reason of the undeveloped heart the English have thrown away the possibility of holding India. For want of a smile an Empire is to be lost. Not even justice is enough. " 'Indians know whether they are liked or not,' " Fielding says, " '—they cannot be fooled here. Justice never satisfies them, and that is why the British Empire rests on sand,' " Mrs. Moore listens to Ronny defending the British attitude; "his words without his voice might have impressed her, but when she heard the self-satisfied lilt of them, when she saw the mouth moving so complacently and competently beneath the little red nose, she felt, quite illogically, that this was not the last word on India. One touch of regret—not the canny substitute but the true regret—would have made him a different man, and the British Empire a different institution."

Justice is not enough then, but in the end neither are liking and goodwill enough. For although Fielding and Aziz reach out to each other in friendship, a thousand little tricks of speech, a thousand different assumptions and different tempi keep them apart. They do not understand each other's *amounts* of emotion, let alone kinds of emotion. " 'Your emotions never seem in proportion to their objects, Aziz,' " Fielding says, and Aziz answers, " 'Is emotion a sack of potatoes, so much the pound, to be measured out?' "

The theme of separateness, of fences and barriers, the old theme of the Pauline epistles, which runs through all Forster's novels, is, in *A Passage to India,* hugely expanded and everywhere dominant. The separation of race from race, sex from sex, culture from culture, even of man from himself, is what underlies every relationship. The separation of the English from the Indians is merely the most dramatic of the chasms in this novel. Hindu and Moslem cannot really approach each other; Aziz, speaking in all friendliness to Professor Godbole, wishes that Hindus did not remind him of cow-dung and Professor Godbole thinks, " 'Some Moslems are very violent' "—"Between people of distant climes there is always the possibility of romance, but the various branches of Indians know too much about each other to surmount the unknowable easily." Adela and Ronny cannot meet in sexuality, and when, after the trial, Adela and Fielding meet in an idea, "a friendliness, as of dwarfs shaking hands, was in the air." Fielding, when he marries Mrs. Moore's daughter Stella, will soon find himself apart from his young wife. And Mrs. Moore is separated from her son, from all people, from God, from the universe.

This sense of separateness broods over the book, pervasive, symbolic— at the end the very earth requires, and the sky approves, the parting of Aziz and Fielding—and perhaps accounts for the remoteness of the characters: they are so far from each other that they cannot reach us. But the isolation is not merely adumbrated; in certain of its aspects it is very precisely analysed and some of the most brilliant and virtuose parts of the novel are devoted to the delineation of Aziz and his friends, to the investigation of the cultural differences that keep Indian and Englishman apart.

The mould for Aziz is Gino Carella of the first novel. It is the mould of unEnglishness, that is to say, of volatility, tenderness, sensibility, a hint of cruelty, much warmth, a love of pathos, the desire to please even at the cost of insincerity. Like Gino's, Aziz's nature is in many ways child-like, in many ways mature: it is mature in its acceptance of child-like inconsistency. Although eager to measure up to English standards of puritan rectitude, Aziz lives closer to the literal facts of his emotions; for good or bad, he is more human. He, like his friends, is not prompt, not efficient, not neat, not really convinced of western ideas even in science—when he retires to a native state he slips back to mix a little magic with his medicine—and he, like them, is aware of his faults. He is hypersensitive, imagining slights even when there are none because there have actually been so many; he is full of humility and full of contempt and desperately wants to be liked. He is not heroic but his heroes are the great chivalrous emperors, Babur and Alamgir. In short, Aziz is a member of a subject race. A rising nationalism in India may by now have thrust him aside in favour of a more militant type; but we can be sure that if the new type has repudiated Aziz's emotional contradictions it has not resolved them.

Aziz and his friends are Moslems, and with Moslems of the business and professional class the plot of the novel deals almost entirely. But the story is suffused with Hinduism. It is Mrs. Moore who carries the Hindu theme; it is Mrs. Moore, indeed, who is the story. The theme is first introduced by Mrs. Moore observing a wasp.

> Going to hang up her cloak she found that the tip of the peg was occupied by a small wasp. . . . There he clung, asleep, while jackals in the plain bayed their desires and mingled with the percussion of drums.
> "Pretty dear," said Mrs. Moore to the wasp. He did not wake, but her voice floated out, to swell the night's uneasiness.

This wasp is to recur in Professor Godbole's consciousness when he has left Chandrapore and taken service as director of education in a Hindu native state. He stands, his school quite forgotten—turned into a granary, indeed—and celebrates the birth of Krishna in the great religious festival that dominates the third part of the novel. The wasp is mixed up in his mind—he does not know how it got there in the first place, nor do we—with a recollection of Mrs. Moore.

> He was a Brahman, she a Christian, but it made no difference, it made no difference whether she was a trick of his memory or a telepathic appeal. It was his duty, as it was his desire, to place himself in the position of the God and to love her, and to place himself in her position and say to the God: "Come, come, come, come." This was all he could do. How inadequate! But each according to his own capacities, and he knew that his own were small. "One old Englishwoman and one little, little wasp," he thought, as he stepped out of the temple into the grey of a pouring wet morning. "It does not seem much, still it is more than I am myself."

The presence of the wasp, first in Mrs. Moore's consciousness, then in Godbole's, Mrs. Moore's acceptance of the wasp, Godbole's acceptance of Mrs. Moore—in some symbolic fashion, this is the thread of the story of the novel as distinguished from its plot. For the story is essentially concerned with Mrs. Moore's discovery that Christianity is not adequate. In a quiet way, Mrs. Moore is a religious woman; at any rate, as she has grown older she has found it "increasingly difficult to avoid" mentioning God's name "as the greatest she knew." Yet in India God's name becomes less and less efficacious—"outside the arch there seemed always another arch, beyond the remotest echo a silence."

And so, unwittingly, Mrs. Moore has moved closer and closer to Indian ways of feeling. When Ronny and Adela go for an automobile ride with the Nawab Bahadur and the chauffeur swerves at something in the path and wrecks the car, Mrs. Moore, when she is told of the incident, remarks without thinking, " 'A ghost!' " And a ghost it was, or so the Nawab believed, for he had run over and killed a drunken man at that spot nine years before. "None of the English knew of this, nor did the chauffeur; it was a racial secret communicable more by blood than by speech." This "racial secret" has somehow been acquired by Mrs. Moore. And the movement away from European feeling continues: "She felt increasingly (vision or nightmare?) that, though people are important, the relations between them are not, and that in particular too much fuss has been made over marriage; centuries of carnal embracement; yet man is no nearer to understanding man." The occasion of her visit to the Marabar Caves is merely the climax of change, although a sufficiently terrible one.

What so frightened Mrs. Moore in the cave was an echo. It is but one echo in a book which is contrived of echoes. Not merely does Adela Quested's delusion go in company with a disturbing echo in her head which only ceases when she masters her delusion, but the very texture of the story is a reticulation of echoes. Actions and speeches return, sometimes in a better, sometimes in a worse form, given back by the perplexing "arch" of the Indian universe. The recurrence of the wasp is a prime example, but there are many more. If Aziz plays a scratch game of polo with a subaltern who comes to think well of this particular anonymous native, the same subaltern will be particularly virulent in his denunciation of Aziz the rapist, never knowing that the liked and the detested native are the same. If the natives talk about their inability to catch trains, an Englishman's missing a train will make all the trouble of the story. Mrs. Moore will act with bad temper to Adela and with surly indifference to Aziz, but her action will somehow have a good echo; and her children will be her further echo. However we may interpret Forster's intention in this web of reverberation, it gives his book a cohesion and intricacy usually only found in music. And of all the many echoes, the dominant one is the echo that booms through the Marabar cave.

> A Marabar cave had been horrid as far as Mrs. Moore was concerned, for she had nearly fainted in it, and had some difficulty in preventing herself from saying so as soon as she got into the air again. It was natural enough; she had always suffered from faintness, and the cave had become too full, because all their retinue followed them. Crammed with villagers and ser-

vants, the circular chamber began to smell. She lost Aziz and Adela in the dark, didn't know who touched her, couldn't breathe, and some vile naked thing struck her face and settled on her mouth like a pad. She tried to regain the entrance tunnel, but an influx of villagers swept her back. She hit her head. For an instant she went mad, hitting and gasping like a fanatic. For not only did the crush and stench alarm her; there was also a terrifying echo.

Professor Godbole had never mentioned an echo; it never impressed him, perhaps. There are some exquisite echoes in India; . . . The echo in a Marabar cave is not like these, it is entirely devoid of distinction. Whatever is said, the same monotonous noise replies, and quivers up and down the walls until it is absorbed in the roof. "Boum" is the sound as far as the human alphabet can express it, or "bou-oum," or "ou-boum"— utterly dull. Hope, politeness, the blowing of a nose, the squeal of a boot, all produce "boum."

Panic and emptiness—Mrs. Moore's panic had been at the emptiness of the universe. And one goes back beyond Helen Schlegel's experience of the Fifth Symphony in *Howards End*: the negating mess of the cave reminds us of and utterly denies the mess of that room in which Caroline Abbott saw Gino with his child. For then the mess had been the source of life and hope, and in it the little child had blossomed; Caroline had looked into it from the "charnel chamber" of the reception room and the "light in it was soft and large, as from some gracious, noble opening." It is, one might say, a representation of the womb and a promise of life. There is also a child in the mess of the Marabar cave—for the "vile, naked thing" that settles "like a pad" on Mrs. Moore's mouth is "a poor little baby, astride its mother's hip." The cave's opening is behind Mrs. Moore, she is facing into the grave; light from the world does not enter, and the universe of death makes all things alike, even life and death, even good and evil.

The echo began in some indescribable way to undermine her hold on life. . . . It had managed to murmur: "Pathos, piety, courage—they exist, but are identical, and so is filth. Everything exists, nothing has value." If one had spoken of vileness in that place, or quoted lofty poetry, the comment would have been the same—"ou-boum." If one had spoken with the tongues of angels and pleaded for all the unhappiness and misunderstanding in the world, past, present, and to come; for all the misery men must undergo whatever their opinion and position, and however much they dodge or bluff—it would amount to the same. . . . Devils are of the north, and poems can be written about them, but no one could romanticize the Marabar because it robbed infinity and eternity of their vastness, the only quality that accommodates them to mankind. . . . But suddenly at the edge of her mind, religion reappeared, poor little talkative Christianity, and she knew that all its divine words from "Let there be Light" to "It is finished" only amounted to "boum."

"Something snub-nosed, incapable of generosity" had spoken to her—"the undying worm itself." Converse with God, her children, Aziz, is repugnant to her. She wants attention for her sorrow and rejects it when given. Knowing Aziz to be innocent, she says nothing in his behalf except a few sour words that upset Adela's certainty, and though she knows that her testimony will be useful to Aziz, she allows Ronny to send her away. She has had the beginning of the Hindu vision of things and it has crushed her. What the Hindu vision is, is expressed by Professor Godbole to Fielding:

> Good and evil are different, as their names imply. But, in my own humble opinion, they are both of them aspects of my Lord. He is present in the one, absent in the other, and the difference between presence and absence is great, as great as my feeble mind can grasp. Yet absence implies presence, absence is not non-existence, and we are therefore entitled to repeat: "Come, come, come, come."

Although Mrs. Moore abandons everything, even moral duty, she dominates the subsequent action. As "Esmiss Esmoor" she becomes, to the crowd around the courthouse, a Hindu goddess who was to save Aziz. And, we are vaguely given to understand, it is her influence that brings Adela to her senses and the truth. She recurs again, together with the wasp, in the mind of Professor Godbole in that wonderful scene of religious muddlement with which the book draws to its conclusion. She remains everlastingly in the mind of Aziz who hates—or tries to hate—all the other English. She continues into the future in her daughter Stella, who marries Fielding and returns to India, and in her son Ralph. Both Stella and Ralph "like Hinduism, though they take no interest in its forms" and are shy of Fielding because he thinks they are mistaken. Despite the sullen disillusionment in which Mrs. Moore died, she had been right when she had said to Ronny that there are many kinds of failure, some of which succeed. No thought, no deed in this book of echoes, is ever lost.

It is not easy to know what to make of the dominant Hinduism of the third section of the novel. The last part of the story is frankly a coda to the plot, a series of resolutions and separations which comment on what has gone before—in it Fielding and Aziz meet and part, this time for ever; Aziz forgives Adela Quested and finds a friend in Ralph Moore; Fielding, we learn, is not really at one with his young wife; Hindu and Moslem, Brahman and non-Brahman are shown to be as far apart as Indian and English, yet English and Moslem meet in the flooded river, in a flow of Hindu religious fervour; and everything is encompassed in the spirit of Mrs. Moore, mixed up with a vision of the ultimate nullity, with the birth of Krishna and with joy in the fertile rains.

Certainly it is not to be supposed that Forster finds in Hinduism an answer to the problem of India; and its dangers have been amply demonstrated in the case of Mrs. Moore herself. But here at least is the vision in which the arbitrary human barriers sink before the extinction of all things. About seventy-five years before *A Passage to India,* Matthew Arnold's brother, William Delafield Arnold, went out to India as Director of Public Education of the Punjab. From his experiences he wrote a novel, *Oakfield: Or, Fellowship in the East;* it was a bitter work which denounced the English for making India a "rupee mine" and it declared that the "grand work" of civilizing India was all humbug. William Arnold thought that perhaps socialism, but more likely the Church of England, could bring about some change. This good and pious man felt it "grievous to live among men"— the Indians—"and feel the idea of fraternity thwarted by facts"; he believed that "we must not resign ourselves, without a struggle, to calling the Indians brutes." To such a pass has Christianity come, we can suppose Forster to be saying. We must suffer a vision even as dreadful as Mrs. Moore's if by it the separations can be wiped out. But meanwhile the separations exist and Aziz in an hysteria of affirmation declares to Fielding on their last ride that the British must go, even at the cost of internal strife, even if it means a Japanese conquest. Only with the British gone can he and Fielding be friends. Fielding offers friendship now: "It's what I want. It's what you want." But the horses, following the path the earth lays for them, swerve apart; earth and sky seem to say that the time for friendship has not come, and leave its possibility to events.

The disintegrating question, What, then, must be done? which many readers have raised is of course never answered—or not answered in the language in which the question has been asked. The book simply involves the question in ultimates. This, obviously, is no answer; still, it defines the scope of a possible answer, and thus restates the question. For the answer can never again temporize, because the question, after it has been involved in the moods and visions of the story, turns out to be the most enormous question that has ever been asked, requiring an answer of enormous magnanimity. Great as the problem of India is, Forster's book is not about India alone; it is about all of human life.

Two Passages to India:
Forster as Victorian and Modern

Malcolm Bradbury

There are major writers whose work seems to us important as a contribution to the distinctive powers and dimensions of art; there are others whose work represents almost a personal appeal to value, and who therefore live— for certain of their readers, at least—with a singular force. There have not been many English novelists of our own time who have established with us the second function, but E. M. Forster is certainly one of them. He has served as an embodiment of the virtues he writes about; he has shown us their function and their destiny; he has left, for other writers and other men, a workable inheritance. Partly this is because he has always regarded art as a matter of intelligence as well as passion, honesty as well as imagination. In making such alliances he has given us a contemporary version of a once-familiar belief—that art can be a species of active virtue as well as a form of magic—and has thus sharply appealed to our sense of what man can be. Literary humanist qualities of this sort are not always easy to express today within the impersonal context of modern literary criticism— which tends, more and more, to ascribe virtue to structural performance within the text and to neglect what lies beyond. In fact, they are crucial virtues, and we fortunately have enough personal testimony—particularly from writers like Christopher Isherwood and Angus Wilson—to see the kind of inheritance he has left. At the same time, what Tony Tanner has called the "trace of totemism" with which Forster has been and is still regarded—and I must assert here my own sense of indebtedness, intellectual,

From *Aspects of E. M. Forster,* edited by Oliver Stallybrass. © 1969 by Edward Arnold Publishers Ltd.

moral, and literary—has its dangers, and to his role and his influence may be ascribed certain slightly odd and uneasy features of Forster's present reputation. That he is a major writer I have no doubt, yet criticism has repeatedly expressed an unsureness about him, has wondered, time and time again, whether he really stands with the other great writers of the century we feel sure of—with Joyce or Conrad or Lawrence.

Why is this? One reason is surely that Forster stands much exposed to our modern predilection for historicist thinking—our inclination to substitute, in Karl Popper's phrase, "historical prophecy for conscience." Forster once told us that he belongs to "the fag-end of Victorian liberalism," and the phrase is often taken with complete literalness and applied against him. As a result his intellectual and his literary destiny has been too readily linked with that strange death of liberal England which historians have dated around 1914, when the equation of economic individualism with social progress lost political force. Since it is easy to explain the exhaustion of political liberalism as a historical necessity, as the inevitable failure of a synthesis proven unworkable by the new social conditions of the second-stage Industrial Revolution, then it is also possible to see Forster's ideas and faith as historically superannuated, too. This view, indeed, has taken root—even though Forster recognises the ironies of the situation and works with them, even though he raises all the crucial questions about elevating social determinism above value; and we often overlook the fact that the liberalism he speaks for so obliquely has had a longer history as a moral conviction than as a political force, that it has as much to do with our idea of man and culture as with our political solutions, that it speaks for a recurrent need for the criticism of institutions and collectivities from the standpoint of the claims of human wholeness. But coupled with this there has been another distrust: distrust of the entire idea of art and culture as Forster suggests or expresses it.

In this century critics have increasingly accepted modernist norms for the judgment of literature, even though, of course, many of our writers have not been modernists in the strict sense. Forster is a paradox here; he is, and he is not. There is in his work the appeal to art as transcendence, art as the one orderly product, a view that makes for modernism; and there is the view of art as a responsible power, a force for belief, a means of judgment, an impulse to spiritual control as well as spiritual curiosity. The point perhaps is that Forster is not, in the conventional sense, a modernist, but rather a central figure of the transition into modernism; and that is surely his interest, the force of his claim. He is, indeed, to a remarkable degree, the representative of two kinds of mind, two versions of literary possibility, and of the tensions of consciousness that exist between them. He stands at the beginning of the age of the new, speaking through it and against it. In this way his five novels—and particularly his last two—can be taken as reflecting the advantages and disadvantages of the humanist literary mind in an environment half hostile to it; they clearly and often painfully carry the strain of a direct encounter with new experience. Forster has been, by training and temperament, sufficiently the historian to see the irony: that culture itself is in history, that a humanist view of the arts as a way of sanely perceiving and evaluating is itself conditioned, for it has its own social environment and limits. So Forster is at once the spokesman for the transcendent symbol, the luminous wholeness of the work of art, out of time and in infinity, and for its obverse—the view that a proper part of art's responsibility is to know and live in the contingent world of history.

If Forster is indeed a Victorian liberal, as some of his critics charge, he is also deeply marked by the encounters that the moralised romantic inheritance must make with those environments which challenge it in matters of belief, technique, and aesthetics. Of course, Forster's confession that he belongs to the fag-end of Victorian liberalism does express a real inheritance; but that end is also the beginning of new forms of belief and of new literary postures and procedures. My point is that he emerges not as a conventionally modernist writer, but rather as a writer who has experienced the full impact of what modernism means—a hope for transcendence, a sense of apocalypse, and *avant-garde* posture, a sense of detachment, a feeling that a new phase of history has emerged—while retaining (with tentative balance that turns often to the ironic mode) much that modernism would affront.

Forster's traditional literary inheritance, which reaches back through the Victorian period to roots in English romanticism, is something which he himself has sketched clearly and well in books like *Marianne Thornton*. He has shown us the formative influence of the world of the Victorian upper-middle-class intelligentsia in its liberal radical mode—that world of "philanthropists, bishops, clergy, members of parliament, Miss Hannah More" which reached into evangelical Christianity and into agnostic enlightenment, that world which he draws upon and values, and against which he also reacts. To the cultural historian, its interest lies in its unconditioned spirit, its sense of disinterestedness, its capacity to act beyond both self and class interest and to transcend its economic roots without losing its social standing. Its view of the critical intelligence working in society is therefore accompanied by no strong sense of disjunction, and it takes many of its terms from the moralised line of English romantic thought. What Forster inherits from it is apparent—something of the flavour of that engaging marriage made by the most influential English romantics, Wordsworth and Coleridge in particular, between the claims on the one hand of the imagination and the poet's transcendent vision, and on the other of right reason and moral duty; something of its power, therefore, to make a vision of Wholeness which embraces the social world in all its contingency. So the personal connection between inner and outer worlds—a connection forged through the powers of passion and imagination—has its social equivalent, in the notion of an obligation on society that it, too, be whole; that it grant, as Mill stresses, "the absolute and essential importance of human development in its richest diversity," that it sees, in Arnold's terms, that perfection can be both an *inward* condition of mind and spirit and a *general* expansion of the human family. Forster draws on the full equation for his fiction, taking as his proper field the social realm of action as well as the life of individuals in their personal relations, and criticising his characters and their society now from the standpoint of right reason and culture, now from that of the heart, the passions, the power of visionary imagination that can testify, however inadequately, to the claims of the infinite. Thus there come under fire "the vast armies of the benighted, who follow neither the heart nor the brain"; and the connective impulses embrace not only man and man, and man and infinity, but the social order, too.

But if Forster is undoubtedly an inheritor of that world of value, he inherits with a due sense of difficulty. In *Howards End* he touches in with deep force those powers and forces in history which are process, and can't be gainsaid; the pastoral and vividly felt landscape of England is turned by the demanding processes of urbanisation and industrialism into a civilisation of luggage; while the very economics of the intelligentsia he belongs to become a matter for ironic exposure. In *A Passage to India* the final nullity of romanticism is exposed in the cave, where the world within us and without echo together the sound of *boum;* this is the extreme beyond Coleridgean dejection, for the visionary hope is lost in the face of an unspeaking and utterly alien nature, a nature only self-reflecting. The will to vision and the liberal thrust to right reason, the desire to connect both with infinity and all mankind, are placed against unyielding forces in nature and history— obstructing the movement of Forster's visionary themes and producing, particularly in these two last novels, a countervailing, ironic reaction. This countervailing sense, this sense of historical apocalypse coupled with spiritual abyss, is surely recognisably modernist. And what in the early novels appears as a species of social comedy—a comedy exercising the claims of moral realism against the liberal wish to draw clear lines between good and bad action—emerges in these latter novels as an essential irony of structure: indeed, as a direct challenge to the values Forster is so often supposed to represent. If, to cite Lionel Trilling (who writes so well of this ironic aspect of Forster), there is an ironic counterpart in the early work whereby while "the plot speaks of clear certainties, the manner resolutely insists that nothing can be quite so simple," these complexities increase in the later work into the mental and aesthetic possession of two colliding views of the world.

Forster's way of assimilating two modes of thought—one an inheritance, the other an urgent group of ideas about contemporary necessity—is matched by the curious aesthetic implications of his techniques in fiction. He is often considered as a writer technically a coeval of his Victorian predecessors (Walter Allen calls him "a throwback"), and in asserting his own debts has particularly named three writers: Jane Austen, Samuel Butler, and Marcel Proust. The indebtedness to the first two of his species of moralised social irony hardly needs elaborating; it is the third name which suggests that the "traditionalist" account of his technique is misleading. Of course, in his novels the omniscient author mediates, with the voice of the guidebook or essay or sermon, the proffered material—though as much to sustain fiction's place in the field of intelligence and thought as to establish the authenticity of fact. But at the same time he offers his work as the symbolist or autotelic artefact; a work of art is "the only material object in the universe which may possess internal harmony." What is so fascinating about his most extended aesthetic statement, *Aspects of the Novel,* is its attempt to place the modes of symbolism and post-impressionism in the context of what might be considered the more "traditional" story-telling function; the novel *tells* (rather than *is*) a story, and it lives in the conditioned world of stuff, of event, of history. (So, finally, Forster puts Tolstoy above Proust.) Yet it has transcendent purposes; art, "the one orderly product which our muddling race has produced," has Platonic powers to touch infinity, reach to the unity behind all things, prophesy (in the Shelleyan sense).

In this respect Forster is as post-impressionist or post-Paterian as anyone else in Bloomsbury, and the ultimate field of action for the arts is that of the "unseen." Procedurally this symbolist power seems to lie in the analogue with music, and is gained from aspects of the novel outside and beyond story, in thematic recurrences, leitmotifs, pattern and rhythm, prophetic song. The problem of whether art can redeem life by transcending it is crucial to modernism; the encounter between the formally transcendent—the epiphany, the unitary symbol—and the world of history recurs throughout its works. And Forster's view is, like that of most modernism, dualistic: art may reach beyond the world of men and things—the world of "story"—but it can never leave that world behind, and must seek meanings and connections in it. What distinguishes Forster is the faint hope which he entertains on behalf of history: the hope that by understanding and right relationship men may win for it a limited redemption.

I have suggested that Forster is deeply involved in some of the largest intellectual, cultural, and aesthetic collisions that occur in the transition into this century; and it is his sharp sense of the contingent, of the powers that rule the world of men, that makes him so. The result is a complex version of modern literary disquiet. An intermediary between those two literary traditions of "moderns" and "contemporaries" that Stephen Spender sees as the two main lines of modern English writing, he bears these burdens so as to expose the crucial choices that a writer of this transitional period might make. Divided as he is between infinite and contingent, he is nonetheless more available to the offered pressures than most of the more confirmed modernists. This is because his sense of the "crisis" of infinity is so much bound up with his sense of the divisive and changing forces of the world of time. For he is increasingly concerned with the problems of the infinite view within the cultural movements of the modernising world; and in his growing sense of the need to synthesise an ever more eclectic experience he testifies to the new multiverse, the chaotic welter of values, which has confounded the modern mind. Hence his visions, though they may suggest an order or unity in the universe, are defined, increasingly from novel to novel, in terms of an anarchy that they must always comprehend. Thus they are never fully redemptive, since the world of time persistently enlarges our feelings of intellectual, moral, social, and spiritual relativism, creating a world in which no one philosophy or cosmology accounts for the world order—where it is possible to believe with Mrs. Moore that "Everything exists; nothing has value." This, with its suggestion that in seeing life whole one may see nothing except multiplicity, is the obverse of the unitary vision; and in *A Passage to India,* his fullest and most eclectic book, Forster gives us in full that possibility—and its sources in social relations, personal relations, and the realm of spirit.

Forster may have an ideal of unity, a will to a whole solution, but we mistake him if we see only that in him. For he is characteristically not a novelist of solutions, but rather of reservations, of the contingencies and powers which inhibit spirit. The power of sympathy, understanding, and community with all things is for him an overriding power; but its claim to wholeness is always conditioned, and mystery, to which we must yield, co-exists with muddle, which we must try to redeem, or even accept in its nullity. Indeed, it is because Forster is so attentive to the forces in our culture and world-order which induce the vision of anarchy—and threaten through its very real powers not only the will to but the very insights of the whole vision—that he seems so central a writer; a novelist whom we in our turn have not always seen whole.

Forster is a difficult and ambiguous writer, a writer who has often made his critics uneasy and caused them to feel how strangely elusive his work is. His observation of his materials, and his way of making his structures, usually involves two tones that come into perplexing relationship. There is the instinct towards "poetry," which goes with the view of art as a symbolist unity; and there is the comedy and the irony, the belittling aspect of his tone, which brings in the problems and difficulties of the contingent world. Because of this it is often possible simultaneously to interpret his work positively and negatively, depending on the kind of critical attentiveness one gives.

Thus for some critics, like Wilfred Stone, *A Passage to India* is Forster's most affirmative and optimistic novel, the one which most suggests, as Stone puts it, that "unity and harmony are the ultimate promises of life." "The theme which this book hammers home," says Stone, "is that, for all our differences, we are in fact *one*. . . . Physically of one environment, we are also psychically one, and it is reason's denial of our commonality, the repression of that *participation mystique,* which has caused man to rule his Indias and himself with such futility and blindness." But other critics like James McConkey and Alan Wilde have come to precisely the opposite view, seeing the work as a novel of the final dissociation between the chaotic life of man and an intractable eternal reality. In part the decision depends upon whether one insists, like Trilling, on a relatively realistic reading of the book, or whether, as E. K. Brown does, one reads it as a "symbolist" novel. If the world of men and manners, of politics and human behaviour, which it depicts suggests divisiveness, the world of the work itself as single "orderly product" suggests profound correspondences within it, a power to resolve its meanings which lies beyond any given character. Of this aspect of the book, Frank Kermode has remarked that it depends upon faking—faking a universe of promised wholeness, of rhetorical and structural unity, of a testing of the world of men from the standpoint of total coherence: "All that civilisation excepts or disconnects has to be got in for meaning to subsist." What this means is that the world of men and the world of order must exist in paradoxical relationship, and this is what Lionel

Trilling seems to imply, too, when he remarks that the novel has an unusual imbalance between plot and story: "The characters are of sufficient size for the plot; they are not large enough for the story—and that indeed is the point of the story." But it is typically in such contrasts of time and transcendence that Forster deals, and to clarify the relationship between them one needs to look very closely at the overall working of the novel.

To a considerable extent, the book deals in themes and matters we have learned to associate with Forster from his previous novels. Here again are those rival claims upon men and nature which dichotomise the universe—the claims of the seen and the unseen, the public and the private, the powers of human activities and institutions and of the ultimate mysteries for which the right institutions and activities have yet to be found. And here again Forster's own sympathies are relatively apparent. The book is focused upon the testing-field of human relationships, with their various possibilities and disasters; on the "good will plus culture and intelligence" which are the necessary conditions of honest intercourse; on the clashes of interest and custom which divide men but which the liberal mind must hope, as fielding hopes, to transcend. Its modes of presentation are familiarly complex—moving between a "poetic" evocation of the world of mystery and a "comic" evocation of the world of muddle, which is in a sense its obverse and refers to the normal state of men.

But what is unmistakable, I think, is that in this book Forster reveals new powers and resources— of a kind not previously achieved in his fiction—and that this extension of resource is linked with an extension of his sensibility, and above all with a new sense of complexity. For instance, *A Passage to India* is not simply an international novel—in the Jamesian sense of attempting to resolve contrasting value-systems by means of a cosmopolitan scale of value—but a global novel. The contrast of England and India is not the end of the issue, since India is schismatic within itself; India's challenge is the challenge of the multiverse, a new version of the challenge that Henry Adams faced on looking at the dynamo. What the city is as metaphor in *Howards End,* India is in *Passage;* it is a metaphor of contingency. Forster is not simply interested in raising the social-comic irony of confronting one social world with the standards of another; he stretches through the social and political implications to religious and mystical ones, and finally to the most basic question of all—how, in the face of such contingency, one structures meaning.

The geographical scale of the novel is, in short, supported by a vast scale of standpoint. Forster attempts a structure inclusive of the range of India, and the judgments of the book are reinforced by the festivals and

rituals of three religions, by the heterodoxy—racial, political, cultural, religious, and mystical—of this multiple nation, and by the physical landscape
of a country which both invites meaning ("Come, come") and denies any.
"Nothing embraces the whole of India, nothing, nothing," says Aziz; the
landscape and the spirit of the earth divide men ("Trouble after trouble
encountered him [Aziz], because he had challenged the spirit of the Indian
earth, which tries to keep men in compartments"; and even the sects are
divided within themselves just as the earth is:

> The fissures in the Indian soil are infinite: Hinduism, so solid
> from a distance, is riven into sects and clans, which radiate and
> join, and change their names according to the aspect from which
> they are approached.

Forster's social comedy works to provoke, among a variety of different
and sympathetically viewed groups, those ironic international and intra-
national encounters that come when one value-system meets another and
confusion and muddle ensue. But his other aim is to call up, by a poetic
irradiation, the ironies lying within the forces of mystery and muddle in
the constituted universe of nature itself. For here, too, are deceptions, above
all in the absence of Beauty, which is traditionally a form for infinity, so
that the very discourse of Romanticism becomes negative under the hot
sun—who is "not the unattainable friend, either of men or birds or other
suns, [who] was not the eternal promise, the never-withdrawn suggestion
that haunts our consciousness; he was merely a creature, like the rest, and
so debarred from glory." There is much in India that invites a cosmic
meaning, but it places both man and infinity:

> Trees of a poor quality bordered the road, indeed the whole
> scene was inferior, and suggested that the countryside was too
> vast to admit of excellence. In vain did each item in it call out,
> "Come, come." There was not enough god to go round. The
> two young people conversed feebly and felt unimportant.

All this stretches the Whitmanesque enterprise called up by the title to
a vast level of inclusiveness. It also involves Forster in a placing of the social
and human world of his novel in a way he has never approached before.
One way of putting the situation is to say that the human plot of the novel
is set into singular relation to the verbal plot, with its radiating expansiveness
of language. The human plot of the novel is essentially a story hinging on
Adela Quested, who comes to India to marry, has doubts about her marriage
when she sees what India has made of her fiancé, and tries herself to create

a more reasonable relationship between British and Indians. She takes part in an expedition, arranged by an Indian, to the Marabar caves, in one of which she believes she is attacked by him. She accuses him of attempted rape, and, although at the trial she retracts her accusation, the incident has sown dissent and discord, and has exposed the political and institutional tensions of the country.

The plot moves us from the world of personal relationships to the social world (which in this case involves political relationships), and is set largely in and around the city of Chandrapore, at a time not stated but evidently intended to be in the 1920s. The dense social world that Forster delineates so skilfully consists primarily of racial or religious groups with their own customs and patterns. The English, whom we see largely through the eyes of Adela Quested and Mrs. Moore, visiting India together, are identified with their institutional functions. Mostly professional middle-class people, they have gone through a process of adaptation to their duties, which are, as Ronnie says, "to do justice and keep the peace." They have learned the importance of solidarity, conventions, rank, and standoffishness; and their judgments and their social order are those of a particular class in a particular situation. Their ethics are dutiful and serious; they have a deep sense of rational justice; they are distrustful of mysticism and lethargy; their deep Englishness has been reinforced by their situation. They operate at the level of political and social duty, and their relationships—the ties that bind the characters together and enable Forster to thread the way from one to another—are those of the political and social roles they play.

The other group, which we see first largely through the eyes of Aziz, consists of Indians, though these are themselves divided by religions and castes. Here again what we see are primarily the professional classes, linked to the British by their duties and to their own people by their familial and friendly relationships. The two main groupings that emerge here are, of course, the Hindus and the Moslems, and Forster differentiates carefully between them, and their respective versions of India. Where they differ radically from the English is in their long and adaptive response to the confusions of their country, a response which obscures the firm lines of value that the British in their isolation can protect, and permits lethargy, emotionalism, and mysticism. Forster explores Indian custom and faith in great detail, noting its own patterns of classification, its own way of making and not making social and moral distinctions, above all recognising that Indians have adapted to a different physical environment by being com-prehensive or passive rather than orderly or rationalistic.

These worlds—Anglo-Indian (to use the phrase of the day), Hindu,

Moslem—are given us in full as they connect and draw apart, and Forster enters imaginatively into each of them. And to a large extent what interests him is not the relations between people, the normal matter for the novelist, but their separation. In the novel's social scenes we are always conscious of those who are absent, and much of the discussion in the early part of the novel is devoted to those not present—the whites are talked of by the Indians, the Indians by the whites. And this suggests the vast social inclusiveness of the novel, which spreads beyond the communities established for the sake of the action into a cast of thousands: nameless marginal characters who appear for a moment and are gone, like the punkah wallah or the voice out of the darkness at the club, and the inhabitants of Chandrapore who seem made "of mud moving."

Out of this complex social world derives a complex moral world, in which the values of no one group are given total virtue. The English may have thrown the net of rationalism and "civilisation" over the country, but India's resistance to this—"The triumphant machine of civilisation may suddenly hitch and be immobilised into a car of stone"—puts them in ironic relation to Indian reality; they scratch only the surface of its life, and theirs is a feeble invasion. On the other hand, the passive comprehensiveness of India is seen as itself a kind of social decay, debased as well as spiritual, leading to a potential neglect of man. The traditional repositories of Forsterian virtue—goodwill plus culture and intelligence—function only incompletely in this universe; and Forster's own liberal passion for social connection motivates a large section of the action, but does not contain its chief interest. In the deceptively guidebookish opening chapter Forster establishes an appeal beyond the social world, to the overarching sky; it looks, at first, like a figure for the potential unity of man, the redemption that might come through breaking out of the social institutions and classifications that segregate them into their closed groupings, but the gesture has an ambiguous quality. The civil station "shares nothing with the city except the overarching sky," but the sky itself is an infinite mystery, and reaching away into its "farther distance, . . . beyond colour, last freed itself from blue." Certainly, beyond the world of social organisation is that world of "the secret understanding of the heart" to which Aziz appeals; this is the world that is damaged when Ronnie and Mrs. Moore discuss Aziz and she finds: "Yes, it was all true, but how false as a summary of the man; the essential life of him had been slain."

Forster is, as usual, superb at creating that "essential life" and showing what threatens it, and much of the book deals with its virtues and its triumphs. So at one level the social world *is* redeemed by those who resist its classifications—by Adela and Mrs. Moore, Fielding, Aziz, Godbole. Forster does not belittle their victories directly except in so far as he sees their comedy. But he does place beyond them a world of infinitude which is not, here, to be won through the personal. For this is not the entire realm of moral victory in the novel; indeed, these acts of resistance, which provide the book's lineal structure, are usually marked by failure. Adela's is a conventional disaster; she makes the moral mistake of exposing the personal to the social. Fielding's is more complicated; he is an agent of liberal contact through goodwill plus culture and intelligence, but he, like Mrs. Moore, meets an echo:

> "In the old eighteenth century, when cruelty and injustice raged, an invisible power repaired their ravages. Everything echoes now; there's no stopping the echo. The original sound may be harmless, but the echo is always evil." This reflection about an echo lay at the verge of Fielding's mind. He could never develop it. It belonged to the universe that he had missed or rejected. And the mosque missed it too. Like himself, those shallow arcades provided but a limited asylum.

As for Mrs. Moore, who does touch it, she encounters another force still—the moral nihilism that comes when the boundary walls are down. Her disaster dominates the novel, for it places even moral and mystical virtue within the sphere of contingency; it, too, is subject to spiritual anarchy. Beyond the world of the plot, the lineal world of consequences and relationships, there lies a second universe of fictional structure, which links spiritual events, and then a third, which in turn places these in history and appeals to the infinite recession of the universe beyond any human structure that seeks to comprehend it.

This we may see by noting that in this novel, as compared with the earlier ones, the world of men is clearly granted reduced powers. The universe of time and contingency is made smaller, by the nature that surrounds man, by the scale of the continent on which man's presence is a feeble invasion, by the sky which overarches him and his works. It is a world of dwarfs and of dwarfed relationships, in which the familiar forces of romantic redemption in Forster's work—personal relationships as mirrors to infinity, a willingness to confront the unseen—undertake their movements toward connection without the full support of the universe. The theme recurs, but Mrs. Moore expresses it most strongly in chapter 14, when she reflects on her situation and grows towards her state of spiritual nullity in the cave:

> She felt increasingly (vision or nightmare?) that, though people are important, the relations between them are not, and that in particular too much fuss has been made over marriage; centuries of carnal embracement, yet man is no nearer to understanding man. And today she felt this with such force that it seemed itself a relationship, itself a person who was trying to take hold of her hand.

The negative withdrawal is, of course, an aspect of that "twilight of the double vision in which so many elderly people are involved," and it is not the only meaning in the book. But it is the dominant one. It is by seeking its obverse that Adela compounds her basic moral error:

> It was Adela's faith that the whole stream of events is important and interesting, and if she grew bored she blamed herself severely and compelled her lips to utter enthusiasms. This was the only insincerity in a character otherwise sincere, and it was indeed the intellectual protest of her youth. She was particularly vexed now because she was both in India and engaged to be married, which double event should have made every instant sublime.

Human relationships are dwarfed not only by the scale of the historical and social world, which is potentially redeemable, but by the natural world, which is not.

Of course, intimations of transcendence are present throughout the novel. Structurally they run through the seasonal cycle, from divisive hot sun to the benedictive healing water at the end, and from Mosque to Caves to Temple. By taking that as his order, Forster is able poetically to sustain the hope of a spiritual possibility, a prefiguring of the world beyond in the world below. The climax of this theme is Godbole's attempt at "completeness, not reconstruction." But what happens here is that divine revelation is shifted to the level of the comic sublime; Forster's rhetoric now puts what has been spiritually perplexing—the webs, nets, and prisons that divide spirit as well as society—back into the comic universe of muddle. The Mau festival is the celebration of the formlessness of the Indian multiverse, seen for a moment inclusively. The poetic realm of the novel, in which above all Mrs. Moore and Godbole have participated, and which has dominated the book's primary art, is reconciled with the muddle of the world of men, in an emotional cataract that momentarily repairs the divisions of the spiritual world (through Godbole's revelation) and the social world (through the festival itself). It satisfies much of the passion for inclusiveness that has been one thread in the novel, the desire that heaven should include all because India *is* all. Earlier the two Christian missionaries have disagreed: Mr. Sorley, the more advanced,

> admitted that the mercy of God, being infinite, may well embrace all mammals. And the wasps? He became uneasy during the descent to wasps, and was apt to change the conversation. And oranges, cactuses, crystals and mud? and the bacteria inside Mr. Sorley? No, no, this is going too far. We must exclude someone from our gathering, or we shall be left with nothing.

Godbole's universe of spirit is much more inclusive:

> Godbole consulted the music-book, said a word to the drummer, who broke rhythm, made a thick little blur of sound, and produced a new rhythm. This was more exciting, the inner images it evoked more definite, and the singers' expressions became fatuous and languid. They loved all men, the whole universe, and scraps of their past, tiny splinters of detail, emerged for a moment to melt into the universal warmth. Thus Godbole, though she was not important to him, remembered an old woman he had met in Chandrapore days. Chance brought her into his mind while it was in this heated state, he did not select her, she happened to occur among the throng of soliciting images, a tiny splinter, and he impelled her by his spiritual force to that place where completeness can be found . Completeness, not reconstruction. His senses grew thinner, he remembered a wasp seen he forgot where, perhaps on a stone. He loved the wasp equally, he impelled it likewise, he was imitating God. And the stone where the wasp clung—could he . . . no, he could not, he had been wrong to attempt the stone, logic and conscious effort had seduced, he came back to the strip of red carpet and discovered that he was dancing upon it.

His doctrine—"completeness, not reconstruction"—is, of course, a species of transcendence, a momentary vision of the whole, the invocation of a universe invested with spirit. It links up with the symbolist plot of the novel, its power as a radiant image, rather than with plot in the linear sense, with its world of "and then . . . and then. . . ." Threading its way through the novel, to an old woman and a wasp, it takes these "soliciting images" and puts them in new association—not with all things, but with each other and with what else comes almost unbidden into the world of spirit. But the stone is left, and equally spirit may or may not invest the universe in any of its day-to-day affairs: "Perhaps all these things! Perhaps none!" Things, in freeing themselves from their traditional associations, social and historical, form a new order, beyond dialogue, beyond human plot, in the realm where poetic figures function on their own order of consciousness. Yet here, too, irony is at work: mystery is sometimes muddle, completeness is sometimes the universe where "everything exists, nothing has value." If history ultimately obstructs, and does not give us a final, rounded structure in terms of human events, if the horses, the earth, the clutter of human institutions say, "No, not yet," then like obstructions dwell in the realm of spirit and symbol, too: the sky says, "No, not there."

The linear, social plot, then, has stretched a long way in search of a structure of its own that will provide coherence in the world, but if it finds one it is in the form of an oblique, doubtful and ironic promise; personal relations only go so far to solve the muddle of history. As for the symbolist plot, it transcends but it does not redeem; it is there but "neglects to come." The power of the novel lies, of course, in the Whitmanesque ambition to include multitudes, to find eternity in some order in the given world. But is this ambition realised? Intimations of eternity may have their symbols in the world of men (in love and relationship) and in the world of nature (in the force of mystery that resides in things); the social and the natural worlds have in them touches that promise wholeness. But they do not of themselves have unity; they are themselves afflicted by the double vision which is all that man can bring to them, grounded as he is in history and hope at once. The world stretches infinitely about us, and there is infinity beyond us. But questions bring us only to the unyielding hostility of the soil and the unyielding ambiguity of the sky.

The universe, then, is less intimation than cipher; a mask rather than a revelation in the romantic sense. Does love meet with love? Do we receive but what we give? The answer is surely a paradox, the paradox that there are Platonic universals beyond, but that the glass is too dark to see them. Is there a light beyond the glass, or is it a mirror only to the self? The Platonic cave is even darker than Plato made it, for it introduces the echo, and so leaves us back in the world of men, which does not carry total meaning, is just a story of events. The Platonic romantic gesture of the match in the cave is the dominating ambiguity of the book. Does it see *itself* in the polished wall of stone, or is the glimmer of radiance a promise?

> There is little to see, and no eye to see it, until the visitor arrives for his five minutes, and strikes a match. Immediately another flame rises in the depths of the rock and moves towards the surface like an imprisoned spirit: the walls of the circular chamber have been most marvellously polished. The two flames approach and strive to unite, but cannot, because one of them breathes air, the other stone. A mirror inlaid with lovely colours divides the lovers, delicate stars of pink and grey interpose, exquisite nebulae, shadings fainter than the tail of a comet or the midday moon, all the evanescent life of the granite, only here visible. Fists and fingers thrust above the advancing soil—here at last is their skin, finer than any covering acquired by the animals, smoother than windless water, more voluptuous than love. The radiance increases, the flames touch one another, kiss, expire. The cave is dark again, like all the caves.

Isn't it less the transcendence of a Whitman, uniting all things through the self and the ongoing lines of history, than the ambiguous and narcissistic transcendence of Melville, where the universe is a diabolical cipher, where the desire to penetrate meaning ends only in our being swallowed up in the meaning we have conferred? Isn't the novel not Forster's "Passage to India," but rather, in the end, Forster's *Moby-Dick?*

Only Connect . . . : Forster and India

K. Natwar-Singh

As I write this essay affectionate recollections of Mr. Forster come rushing to my mind. I do not wish to drive them away, even though they might make a dispassionate appraisal difficult. Just as he found it impossible to resist India, his friends find it impossible to resist him. I have had the good fortune of calling Mr. Forster a friend for fifteen years; it is largely to him that I owe such awakening as has befallen me. I have said elsewhere that a part of myself, such as I am today, has been moulded and permanently influenced by him. I do not know if that would do him any credit, but without him my life would have been infinitely poorer. His writings and his personal example have made some of his readers aware, if not capable, of higher things. He cured us of some of our baser ambitions and instincts: if, to adapt a familiar saying, we can't beat them we don't want to join them either. The result is that his "aristocracy of the sensitive, the considerate and the plucky" gets short shrift in the rough and tumble of everyday life. Yet it never gives up, never gives in. Its members are to be found in three generations of Indians who have had the pleasure of calling Morgan Forster a friend.

This emotional intimacy and *rapport,* spreading over most of the twentieth century, with a people so different from his own has been achieved through affection, loyalty, a warm heart, and sensitive understanding. He has spoken with a voice unlike anybody else's. The Indore preacher conveys much of our love for Forster when he tells him during the Gokul Ashtami Festival: "We have not met an Englishman like you previously."

From *Aspects of E. M. Forster,* edited by Oliver Stallybrass. © 1969 by Edward Arnold Publishers Ltd.

A meeting of minds may not have always been achieved, but the hearts did meet. The radiance of his triple vision—as friend, critic, creative artist—has helped a few of us in "the building of the rainbow bridge that should connect the prose in us with the passion" so that we might "connect without bitterness until all men are brothers." That is the essence of *A Passage to India,* the reason why it endures. It is still read, not because it found answers "to the tragic problem of India's political future," but because it promotes the creed that without love you cannot "connect." The "undeveloped hearts" which ruled India failed to "connect": their work and labours ended in "panic and emptiness."

In contemporary India Forster is not widely known, and judgment has been passed on him almost wholly on the basis of *A Passage to India. The Hill of Devi* evoked an India that was not popular in the 1950s; in a letter to me in 1954 Forster wrote: "Yes, I am afraid the book will be as uncongenial to the new India as *A Passage* was to the old Anglo-India. The outlook of both the books is much the same. I think it is the political situation that has altered." The later book was misunderstood as an apology for the Princely Order. No one remembered that as long ago as 1922, in his remarkable essay, "The Mind of the Indian Native State," Forster had said: "An alliance between the British and the Princes against the rest of India could only lead to universal disaster, yet there are people on both sides who are foolish enough to want it."

But there is a hard core of admirers who are aware of the deep and powerful influence he had on the moral outlook of his age, and to them he came as a blessed relief after Kipling.

Having mentioned Kipling's name, I must pause and say something about him in relation to Forster. For the first quarter of the twentieth century the English-speaking world, perhaps including Forster, looked at India largely through the eyes of Rudyard Kipling. In his tribute to Ross Masood, Forster says—"Until I met him, India was a vague jumble of rajas, sahibs, babus and elephants, and I was not interested in such jumble: who could be?" Well, a great many Englishmen were, for that is precisely the India which Kipling very nearly succeeded in immortalising. All that tosh about the white man's burden and the stiff upper lip which made the sahibs at Poona and Cheltenham feel so pukka only widened the gulf between India and Britain. Forster, to some extent, provided the corrective, but the damage had been done.

Sensitive Indians found Kipling's jingoism offensive and offending, and many would agree with Orwell's comment that he was "morally insensitive and aesthetically disgusting." Orwell's correction of the "white man's burden" to "black man's burden" is is also very much to the point; for, unlike Forster, Kipling had no understanding of the economics of imperialism or for that matter any kind of economics. It was beyond him to realise or learn that the British Raj, like all other empires, was an exploitation machine. He would have been completely baffled by Martin Luther King's comment that "the peculiar genius of imperialism was found in its capacity to delude so much of the world into the belief that it was civilising primitive cultures even though it was grossly exploiting them."

Forster and his like would neither build nor sustain empires; they have not the dedicated zeal, not the self-righteous, public school sense of responsibility upon which empires rest, as do their graves.

Forster has been to India three times. His first visit was in 1912–13, in the company of Goldsworthy Lowes Dickinson and R. C. Trevelyan. It was during this trip that he met, through Sir Malcolm Darling—a nonestablishment Civil Servant and an exception to the generally unattractive set of men who ruled India—the Maharaja of Dewas Senior, Bapu Sahib, who "was certainly a genius and possibly a saint." During this visit Forster travelled fairly extensively and made many friends. In spite of the bombthrowing incident at Delhi, in which the Viceroy, Lord Hardinge, was slightly injured, the India of 1912 was politically very dull and inactive; and the Indian National Congress, in the words of Jawaharlal Nehru—who had just returned to India after seven years at Harrow, Cambridge, and London—"was very much an English-knowing upper-class affair where morning coats and well-pressed trousers were greatly in evidence. Essentially it was a social gathering with no political excitement of tension." Gandhi was still in South Africa and relatively unknown.

The second visit was from April to November 1921. He spent most of his time at Dewas, where he was private secretary to the Maharaja. It was during this trip that Forster saw "so much of the side of life that is hidden from most English people."

Forster's last visit to India was in 1945, when he came to attend the Indian PEN Conference. His two great friends, Masood and Bapu Sahib, had died in 1937. He travelled to Delhi, Calcutta, Bombay, and Hyderabad. Finally, he visited Santiniketan, "the home and the creation of Tagore. . . . I spent a night there, and understood why it has exercised a mystic influence on many of its sons. You will either know a great deal about Santiniketan or else you will never have heard of it. It is that kind of place. Its name means 'The Home of Peace.' " Tagore, of course, was dead and so was

Iqbal and "their disappearance has impoverished the scene." Forster had met them both and has written about them in *Abinger Harvest* and *Two Cheers for Democracy*. Of this last visit he says:

> The big change I noticed was the increased interest in politics. You cannot understand the modern Indians unless you realise that politics occupy them passionately and constantly, that artistic problems, and even social problems—yes and even economic problems—are subsidiary. Their attitude is "first we must find the correct political solution, and then we can deal with other matters." I think the attitude is unsound, and used to say so; still, there it is, and they hold it much more vehemently than they did a quarter of a century ago. When I spoke about the necessity of form in literature and the importance of the individual vision, their attention wandered, although they listened politely. Literature, in their view, should expound or inspire a political creed.

In pre–1947 India "Art for Art's Sake" was not a popular creed, and understandably so. First the battle for independence had to be won, then the problems of literature could be attended to.

"And did I do any good?" Forster asks himself. "Yes, I did. I wanted to be with Indians, and was, and that is a very little step in the right direction."

Mr. Forster is perhaps the only Englishman, certainly the only English writer, to have inspired half-a-dozen Indian writers to present a book of tributes to him.

In March 1963 Santha Rama Rau and Raja Rao were in my apartment in Manhattan. Santha's dramatisation of *A Passage to India* was still being talked about. Raja Rao's second novel in twenty-five years, *The Serpent and the Rope,* had received attention in serious literary circles in America. Forster's name naturally came up. Raja Rao said I should postpone my "study" of Forster and edit instead an Indian tribute to him as an offering on his eighty-fifth birthday. He added that nobody had done more for his writing than Forster. Both his first novel, *Kanthapura,* and *The Serpent and the Rope* were published with Forster's help, and became successes in their own right. So a decision was taken to get on with the project. Forster gave his affectionate blessing and by permitting inclusion of selections from his Indian writings—among them his virtually unknown but deeply moving and perceptive tribute to Gandhi—made publication possible.

The book, when it appeared, attracted attention in unexpected quarters.

American admirers of Forster and critics responded warmly and it provided them an occasion to join in *A Tribute*. It also provided an opportunity for a reappraisal of Forster's work, its relevance and importance to present-day problems. The *Wall Street Journal,* as befits a sound financial paper, posed the most pertinent question:

> Few men of the West, none of them statesman, or in what C. P. Snow calls the corridors of power, can have had as much praise and of such kind from the East. . . . What was this accomplishment that won such feelings for an Englishman writing as a novelist about India; a circumstance that could have, and often has, engendered hostility?

The accomplishment is indeed of a very high order, possibly unique. On the other hand it has been resolutely private and on the other is has had wider, even universal, overtones. India has been a major but by no means an exclusive influence on Forster, even though he calls his stay in Dewas "the great opportunity of my life."

A Passage to India describes the "human predicament." It also describes an India that has altered very considerably since 1924, but despite subsequent works on India by westerners, it remains the outstanding example of an Englishman's honest effort to understand and interpret this country and its complex people.

My theme, Forster and India, debars me from discussing the artistic and other excellences of *A Passage to India,* and I shall confine myself to its politics, which remained relevant for a very long time. The Indian situation changed, but comparable situations sprang up in other parts of the British Empire, and the same mistakes were made. The insolence of British administrators, the behaviour of their wives, the thoughtless imposition of unworkable federations, continued till only the other day.

What impact, if any, did it make in England forty-five years ago? What impact did it make in India? Forster has himself provided an answer to the first question. In 1962 I asked him what were the Indian and British reactions to *A Passage to India* when it appeared in 1924.

> EMF: For a long time no one took any notice. Then a paper called the *Morning Post* reviewed it favourably. After a year or two it started—the reactions to the book, I mean. I also received a few abusive letters from Anglo-Indians.
>
> Q : What is your own assessment of the political influence it had on the "Indian question" of the time? Do you think its political influence was accidental and exaggerated?

EMF: It had some political influence—it caused people to think of the link between India and Britain and to doubt if that link was altogether of a healthy nature. The influence (political) was not intended; I was interested in the story and the characters. But I welcomed it.

There is no doubt that thoughtful, honest, liberal-minded Englishmen and intellectuals both in the Government and outside began to look at the Indian situation from a different point of view.

The literary intelligentsia were shocked and deeply disturbed. Forster made the British Raj stick in their throats, and it wasn't a comfortable or comforting sensation to live with. Looking beyond and beneath the brilliance of the writing, they began to ask: "What are we up to in India?" As a novelist it was not Forster's responsibility to find political solutions. Morally there could be no justification for one race ruling over another. The problem was posed and an indictment made: the British Raj might win a few battles, but it was losing the war. The English and the Indians could not be friends as long as the Raj lasted. That Indo-British relations took the turn they did during Mountbatten's time is a vindication of what Aziz says to Fielding at the end of the book. Hope was not abandoned; it was only postponed.

Forster was the first English writer to portray Indians as human beings and not merely as caricatures or doubtful and shifty natives. But he is no Indophile. There are indignant and highly critical portions in *Passage* and *Devi*. He noticed and commented on our inattention to detail, our idleness and incompetence. The Hindu's preoccupation with intrigue and suspicion did not go unnoticed. "Intelligent though they are over intrigues, Indians too can get confused and identify hopes with facts. One is reduced—as are they—to siding with the people one likes." He was helpless in the presence of the widespread Hindu habit of referring to almost all religious and metaphysical matters by a periphrasis.

We took it from him (even Godbole's highbrow incoherence) for two reasons. First, because he was harder on his own people, whose reaction, indeed, proved that "nothing enrages Anglo-India more than the lantern of reason if it is exhibited for one moment after its extinction is decreed." Second, because he seems to have taken to heart the words of Tagore: "Come inside India, accept all her good and evil: if there be deformity then try and cure it from within, but see it with your own eyes, understand it, think over it, turn your face towards it, become one with it."

Forster's portrayal of Anglo-India has been disapprovingly commented upon. It has been labelled as exaggerated and uncharitable. But this view does not stand up to close scrutiny. The men who "ruled India" *did* behave badly, *did* snub Indians, while their women "knew none of the politer forms [of Urdu] and of the verbs only the imperative mood." They constantly outraged Indian sentiments. Even after independence sections of the British community in certain cities ran their own clubs on racial lines. Such behaviour was not likely to endear them to a free India any more than that of their fathers had endeared them to Forster.

Does Forster do injustice to the British Civil Servants in India? Is he unfair to them? Let us call Nehru as witness:

> They lived in a narrow, circumscribed world of their own—
> Anglo-India—which was neither England nor India. They had
> no appreciation of the forces at work in contemporary society.
> In spite of their amusing assumption of being the trustees and
> guardians of the Indian masses, they knew little about them and
> even less about new aggressive bourgeoisie. They judged Indians
> from the sycophants and office-seekers who surrounded them
> and dismissed others as agitators and knaves. Their knowledge
> of post-war changes all over the world, and especially in the
> economic sphere, was of the slightest, and they were too much
> in the ruts to adjust themselves to changing conditions. They
> did not realise that the order they represented was out of date
> under modern conditions, and they were approaching as a group
> more and more the type which T. S. Eliot describes in "The
> Hollow Men."

Forster would have been spared a great deal of criticism if more people in India had read Rose Macaulay's comment: "Some confusion is perhaps caused by the book's doubtful chronology, for it deals with the India of one period, is written largely from material collected and from a point of view derived from that period, and was published twelve years later, when Indians and English had got into quite another stage." The "doubtful chronology" of the book did indeed create confusion. It depicts a pre–1914 India and by the time it was published in 1924 events had overtaken it. It appears to be an almost anti-nationalist book, since it makes no mention of the political ferment that was going on in India in the early 1920s.

The First World War had changed everything. The Montagu-Chelmsford reforms had not fully met Indian aspirations, Gandhi had launched his non-cooperation movement, Tagore had renounced his knighthood after General Dyer had killed 379 peaceful Indians in cold blood in Jallianwallah

Bagh. After this, Gandhi, who till then had tolerated the British Raj, became its most outspoken opponent. The book therefore, failed to impress the Indian nationalists, who consisted largely of middle-class intellectuals. It made little or no impact in India. The issues had gone beyond good manners. It succeeded in annoying the British without satisfying Indian political aspirations. Gandhi did not read it, and the highly intelligent and erudite C. Rajagopalachari, the man who succeeded Mountbatten as the first and last Indian Governor-General, did not do so till quite recently. Nehru did, and refers to it in his *Autobiography*.

It seems odd that a person of Forster's awareness could have been so totally oblivious of what was going on in India in 1921. It is typical of him not to have explained, or to have tried to explain it away. We had to wait for *The Hill of Devi* to solve the mystery, and even that only on a very close reading.

In a recent article in *Encounter* Andrew Shonfield says that "Forster had little understanding and no sympathy for the complicated and courageous politics of the Indian independence movement." Forster's political antennae were a little more acute and active than Mr. Shonfield imagines. Writing about the visit of the Prince of Wales in 1921, Forster in places sounds amazingly like Nehru—although this was the year which saw Nehru in prison for the first time.

> About the Prince of Wales's visit I might also write much. It is disliked and dreaded by nearly everyone. The chief exceptions are the motor-firms and caterers, who will make fortunes, and the non-cooperators and extremists, who will have an opportunity for protest which they would otherwise have lacked. . . . The National Congress meets in December at Ahmedabad, and it will certainly carry through its resolution in favour of Civil Disobedience, and if there is general response, this expensive royal expedition will look rather foolish. I have been with pro-Govt and pro-English Indians all this time, so cannot realise the feeling of the other party; and am only sure of this—that we are paying for the insolence of Englishmen *and* Englishwomen out here in the past. I don't mean that good manners can avert a political upheaval. But they can minimise it, and come nearer to averting it in the East than elsewhere. . . . But it's too late. Indians don't long for social intercourse with Englishmen any longer. They have made a life of their own.

Nehru says much the same thing in his *Autobiography* which *The Hill of Devi* preceded by nearly fifteen years.

G. Lowes Dickinson is reported by E. M. Forster, in his recent life of him, to have once said about India: "And *why* can't the races meet? Simply because the Indians *bore* the English. *That* is the simple adamantine fact." It is possible that most Englishmen feel that way and it is not surprising. To quote Forster again (from another book), every Englishman in India feels and behaves, and rightly, as if he was a member of an army of occupation, and it is quite impossible for natural and unrestrained relations between the two races to grow under these circumstances. The Englishman and the Indian are always posing to each other and naturally they feel uncomfortable in each other's company. Each bores the other and is glad to get away from him to breathe freely and move naturally again.

Usually the Englishman meets the same set of Indians, those connected with the official world, and he seldom reaches really interesting people, and if he reached them he would not easily draw them out. The British regime in India has pushed up into prominence, even socially, the official class, both British and Indian, and this class is most singularly dull and narrow-minded. Even a bright young Englishman on coming out to India will soon relapse into a kind of intellectual and cultural torpor and will get cut off from all live ideas and movements. After a day in office, dealing with the ever-rotating and never-ending files, he will have some exercise and then go to his club to mix with his kind, drink whisky and read *Punch* and the illustrated weeklies from England. He hardly reads books and if he does he will probably go back to an old favourite. And for this gradual deterioration of mind he will blame India, curse the climate, and generally anathematise the tribe of agitators who add to his troubles, not realising that the cause of intellectual and cultural decay lies in the hide-bound bureaucratic and despotic system of government which flourishes in India and of which he is a tiny part.

Forster always warmed to talk about Jawaharlal Nehru. He met Nehru twice and recalled these meetings with feeling. Nehru's style, his secularism, his internationalism, his quiet but open agnosticism, all appealed to Forster and he was, even when not wholly approving of the turn the Indian National movement was taking, horrified that men like Gandhi and Nehru should be denied the freedom to say their say. Forster once said to me: "Nehru is the most upright and level-headed statesman in the world. Politicians are

generally busy tidying up their past. Your Prime Minister is an exception."
In 1964, a few weeks after Nehru's death, I gave Forster a copy of Nehru's
last will and testament. Forster was visibly moved and said how saddened
he was at Nehru's passing away. He told an American friend of mine that
he "would have voted for Nehru with both hands."

Forster has also been taken to task for choosing a Moslem as the main
character in his novel. This hasn't worried the Indians too much. Even after
partition sixty million co-religionists of Aziz live in India. Islam is their
religion, India their home. That Aziz had been taken as *the* Moslem and
Godbole as *the* Hindu is unfortunate. It is wrong and dangerous to talk in
such confined terms. Just as there is no such thing as the real India, there
is no single individual representing an entire community. Forster as a novelist and creative artist was free to choose anyone for his hero. His choice
does not make him pro-Moslem or anti-Hindu. The community of the
person was unimportant for describing and highlighting the human predicament, and for human relationships.

Forster himself told me: "I think of them—of Aziz and Godbole—as
people and not as religious types." And I am content to leave it at that.
Forster has many Moslem friends, and a larger number of Hindu friends.
It is a matter of chance and not of calculation.

The Hill of Devi finally nails the lie that Forster does not know his
Hindu well. Even given Forster's insight into human character, his gift for
finding the right words for the right occasions, his talent for uncovering
layer after layer of the human personality, his sturdy moral realism, his
aesthetic sense and his sense of the unseen, no one who had not made a
study of Hindu philosophy and thought could have written such a book.
Raja Rao calls it "one of the most Indian books of this century." Whether
he writes about Hindu or Moslems, he penetrates their hearts and the result
is dazzling. The sheer authenticity of the dialogue in both books is stag-
gering. His description of the Gokul Ashtami festival is flawless. Forster
caught the *spirit* of the festival and found meaning and significance in Hindu
ritual which have eluded or escaped other English writers.

He also took the trouble to study the Bhagavad-Gita. Without such a
study, his description of Gokul Ashtami would have been superficial. A
Hindu festival made him aware of a gap in Christianity: "the canonical
gospels do not record that Christ laughed or played. Can a man be perfect
if he never laughs or plays? Krishna's jokes may be vapid, but they bridge
a gap."

Forster had obviously read the Bhagavad-Gita either before or during
his first visit in 1912. His essay "Hymn before Action" deserves to be better

known. It analyses the central core of the Gita. Krishna asks Arjuna to fight and destroy his enemies even though they be his close relatives. Arjuna must fight because it is his duty and that duty has not been assigned to him by chance. Krishna convinces Arjuna, who drives into battle rejoicing, and wins a great victory. "But it is necessarily and rightly followed by disillusionment and remorse. The fall of his enemies leads to his own, for the fortunes of men are all bound up together, and it is impossible to inflict damage without receiving it."

Forster has acknowledged his debt to India and Indians. It is time we acknowledged our debt to him. Even at the best of times Forster has been aware of the excesses of nationalism and for a long time his attitude to Indian nationalism was cautiously sympathetic, not noisy and erratic like Bertrand Russell's. In spite of hating "causes," he has consistently, quietly, and candidly stood up for India. When many of the professional and loud-mouthed British friends of India looked the other way, he came out strongly in support of India at the time of the Chinese aggression in 1962.

> We can urge on our Government and the Governments of the West to supply arms on lend lease, and to increase the aid they give for India's Plans, now that India's own resources have so largely to be devoted to war. Above all, we must try to give additional heart and courage to our Indian friends whose spirit in the crisis is sound and steadfast. On the survival and success of India depends the hope for a better life of one-fifth of the human race. We cannot let the Chinese aggressors destroy this hope.

During the Second World War, as President of the National Council for Civil Liberties, he took up the cudgels on behalf of Jaya Prakash Narayan, who was being tortured in Lahore jail. He was appalled that his countrymen should treat brave patriots like Jaya Prakash Narayan in this brutal manner.

Since personal relationships are at the centre of Forster's creed, it is appropriate to end on a personal note. Without his support and backing the careers of some of India's leading writers would not have been possible. I have already mentioned Raja Rao and Santha Rama Rau. Mulk Raj Anand told me that in 1935 Forster saved him from suicide by adding a preface to his first novel *Untouchable,* which had been rejected by seventeen publishers. His generous intervention in 1940 for Ahmed Ali's novel *Twilight in Delhi,* his discriminating observations about R. K. Narayan, G. V. Desani, and Narayan Menon illustrate his belief that the Indian talent is no less significant than any other, given the chance. His has been truly "the face of a friend" and what he said of Gandhi is in no small measure applicable to himself:

> He is with all the men and women who have sought something in life that is neither chaos nor mechanism, who have not confused happiness with possessiveness, or victory with success, and who have believed in love.

Language and Silence in *A Passage to India*

Michael Orange

> *Wovon man nicht sprechen kann, darüber muss man schweigen.*
>
> Wittgenstein, *Tractatus*

Forster's delicacy of style in the novels that precede *A Passage to India* almost guarantees the rectitude of his attempt to understand the alien worlds of Islam, Hinduism and "British India." Elements of potential condescension or of patronising naïveté in the class attitudes of some of the characters of *Howards End* are carefully noted by the novelist, a useful starting-point for one whose last-written novel will share their position of attempted understanding. Over fifty years after the first publication of *A Passage to India* it is possible to measure the success of that book in the context of renewed attempts at discovering the relevance for the industrialised nations of cultures whose assumptions have been so different. Forster goes incomparably further than the instinctive refusal to articulate that has often accompanied the quest. Yet *A Passage to India* justifies this disengagement with language. More, it explains, while enacting, the strategy behind such refusals to communicate.

"The Ganges happens not to be holy here." The novel's third sentence thus quietly registers and assimilates a phenomenon unfamiliar except in classical mythology to western readers. The concept that a river may be "holy" coincides, however, with the further understanding that in India, apparently, the same river is, in different locations, religiously speaking "neutral." Yet the phrase's undemonstratively parenthetical tone insinuates

From *E. M. Forster: A Human Exploration: Centenary Essays,* edited by G. K. Das and John Beer. © 1979 by Michael Orange. Macmillan, 1979.

that this is not remarkable. The sense of wonder will be exercised more fully later. In the scale *A Passage to India* plays upon, such differentiation from Western values is scarcely noticed. Nonetheless, it is crucial. As an index of the gap between oriental and western culture the phrase asserts, quite literally, a world of difference: wholly divergent concepts of the universe.

However, even with this abyss confronting western consciousness so early in the novel, a converging movement can be detected. Classical my-thology and Forster's unemphatic tone combine to imply that such an alien world-view may be assimilated at least conceptually. In the act of reading a bridge of some kind has been thrown across. By the third section of the novel, when this continual verbal oscillation between alien and familiar has become a conditioning medium of response, Forster can spin the coin almost carelessly to reveal the common metal on which two different cultures are stamped:

> a Brahman brought forth a model of the village of Gokul (the Bethlehem in that nebulous story) and placed it in front of the altar . . . Here, upon a chair too small for him and with a head too large, sat King Kansa, who is Herod, directing the murder of some Innocents, and in a corner, similarly proportioned, stood the father and mother of the Lord, warned to depart in a dream.

But this is the limit to Forster's cultural parallelism. For *A Passage to India* continually asserts, despite some initiation into concepts of unity, that the images are firmly embedded in history; that the coin is diamond-faceted; and that language itself is powerless to convey the central experience to which the novel leads.

The success of *A Passage to India* depends acutely upon its pervasive sensitivity to its own verbal medium. In this novel the language of cog-nition, as the expression of thought and feeling in hierarchy subject to ordering by time, is avowedly insufficient as a means of incarnating mystical experience which exists outside time and is subversive of hierarchical order. In translating private, inward experience into public, shared understanding, the writer commits himself to materials crudely subject to history, hierarchy and consciousness. Where language encounters the silence beyond "liberal humanism" or conceptualisation itself, it must settle for being signpost rather than analogue. At the point of silence the alternatives for the artist are to retreat into the crudity of words again, or to fail to create at all. Forster's interest in musical expression underlines the point. The conclusion to the biography of Dickinson provides an interesting commentary on the problem, which has special relevance to *A Passage to India:*

> He was an indescribably rare being, he was rare without being enigmatic, he was rare in the only direction which seems to be infinite: the direction of the Chorus Mysticus. He did not merely increase our experience: he left us more alert for what has not yet been experienced and more hopeful about other men because he had lived. And a biography of him, if it succeeded, would resemble him; it would achieve the unattainable, express the inexpressible, turn the passing into the everlasting. Have I done that? *Das Unbeschreibliche hier ist's getan?* No. And perhaps it only could be done through music. But that is what has lured me on.

Such contemporary examples as Eliot's choice of ending for *The Waste Land* and the experimental fictions of Virginia Woolf, Gertrude Stein and Aldous Huxley illuminate Forster's patient understanding of his craft. His achievement in *A Passage to India* is measured in part by his considerable success in transcending those limitations while preserving fidelity to traditional means of expression: the passage is to India, but the importance of the return ticket is not minimised. While the novel is supremely graceful farewell to Forster's art, it is by no means a leave-taking imposed by insufficiency in his manipulation of the form, which proves flexible enough to focus both on the mystery of the tunnel of the stars and on the rigours of "Cousin Kate" as performed in Central India.

This flexibility is paramount in the novel. Forster quietly but insistently induces belief in his verbal structures while disavowing their efficacy. The persistent muting of his ironic tones disinfects the prose of any trace of self-seeking virtuosity and directs attention outward to the ostensible subject matter—which necessarily resides, of course, within the words themselves. This controlling irony at the expense of the fiction itself functions as a continual reminder that any commitment to values expressed through words and based upon the hierarchies that they express must contend with functional limitations. Much experience is resolutely nonverbal. Nonverbal values become progressively and necessarily more remote in proportion to the persuasiveness of the language employed to embody them. The more felicitously they are expressed, the more readily they induce assent to propositions they set out to counter. This fundamental paradox is the source of the novel's classic consequent tension. While language eternally asserts its own reality, one of hierarchy, reason, time, and the logic of emotion, India itself represents a mysterious, sempiternal, mystical reality. Joseph Campbell makes this general point about Eastern culture:

> Throughout the Orient the idea prevails that the ultimate ground of being transcends thought, imaging, and definition. It cannot be qualified. Hence, to argue that God, Man, or Nature is good, just, merciful, or benign, is to fall short of the question. One could as appropriately—or inappropriately—have argued, evil, unjust, merciless, or malignant. All such anthropomorphic predications screen or mask the actual enigma, which is absolutely beyond rational consideration; and yet, according to this view, precisely that enigma is the ultimate ground of being of each and every one of us—and of all things.
>
> Prayers and chants, images, temples, gods, sages, definitions, and cosmologies are but ferries to a shore of experience beyond the categories of thought, to be abandoned on arrival.

The resolution of the dichotomy between language and enigma represents the most complex aspect of Forster's success in the novel. He reconciles an adept manipulation of his verbal structures to the complete insufficiency of language itself, without finding it necessary to rely upon crudity of utterance to make the crucial disavowal of literary expression's congruence to mystical experience. This confident belief in the elastic power of his medium to work in opposed directions at the same time is the hallmark of *A Passage to India*. (It is pertinent to recall in this context that the British established their hegemony in India largely through the imposition of their language.) The power to reconcile disparity, to unify without sacrificing particularity, which the sensitive manipulation of language can command, establishes *A Passage to India*'s status as a still-breathing masterpiece, rather than as a sad but exquisite register of failures.

II

The conflict dramatised and partly resolved in *Howards End*, between the worlds of "telegrams and anger" represented by the Wilcox family and that of sensitive personal relationships incarnated by the Schlegels, is considerably more complicated in *A Passage to India*. The simple plea "only connect" is applicable fundamentally to the abyss between the efficient English and the sensitive Indians they govern. Nonetheless, Aziz's sensitivity is matched (despite the latter's evident limitations) by Fielding. British devotion to rigid class distinction is more than echoed in the triumph of caste represented by the Nawab Bahadur. Aziz, despite his eventual decision to reside in a Hindu native state, is dismayed to find that after all he feels closer to Fielding than to Professor Godbole. Evidently the precarious bridge thrown across to an alien realm of experience by Margaret Schlegel is metaphorically insufficient to the complexity of *A Passage to India*. The very idea is ridiculed in the unsuccessful "Bridge Party" convened to cater to Miss Quested's desire to know the "real" India: "a party to bridge the gulf between East and West; the expression was [the Collector's] own invention, and amused all who heard it." At the end of the novel there is no "marriage" between Aziz and Fielding. Forster's ironic tones, which effectively qualify the sense of kinship expressed in the banter at the Club, hint at the necessity of acknowledging such reservation. It appears that the sole means of attempting to communicate securely with others takes place from within the solipsistic shell of the individual personality. Mrs Moore is no befuddled sentimentalist, but because of rather than despite her sharpness, is sufficiently sure of herself to reach out to Aziz.

On the level of plot, too, as well as of language, this kind of irony is maintained. The subaltern who baits Fielding for his championship of Aziz unknowingly uses the example of his own brief meeting with Aziz to censure the latter's typical presumption. This restates in slightly different fashion Heaslop's mistaken initial pleasure and subsequent shock at his mother's first encounter at the mosque with the Indian. Yet the subaltern's earlier meeting with Aziz on the Maidan is the most graceful bridging of the racial abyss that the novel offers:

> They reined up again, the fire of good fellowship in their eyes. But it cooled with their bodies, for athletics can only raise a temporary glow. Nationality was returning, but before it could exert its poison they parted, saluting each other. "If only they were all like that," each thought.

It is an episode whose comprehensive irony only becomes apparent at the novel's close. Aziz's and Fielding's last ride together painfully echoes this earlier one but expresses no more, despite all their efforts. Guarded friendliness, goodwill allied to circumspection remain after the vistas of instinctive communication and reciprocal affection close off. It seems scant reward.

The language which describes the polo-practice on the Maidan is crisply adequate to its purpose. The metaphors of temperature neatly register both exercise and passion, while the placing and choice of "poison" conveys the disquietingly jarring note which characterises the relationship between the different races implicit in the scene, assimilated at the same time to the placid rhythm of the sentence which acknowledges the weary normalcy of such diseased relations. The passion for clarity and dispassionate observation harmonises with sensitivity to the subtleties of relationships: metaphor and plain-speaking cohere in this unemphatic idiom. Yet the ironies created by the tone of the narration tend disquietingly to subvert the assurance derived from any sense of confederacy with the latter's congenially sceptical outlook. For example, the Nawab Bahadur's social distance from his coreligionists partly endorses the toughly self-protective realism of the general British aloofness from the natives. Switching to the missionaries Graysford and Sorley, this attitude is more directly, if regretfully, sponsored: "perhaps it is futile for men to initiate their own unity, they do but widen the gulfs between them by the attempt." In following the quotation through to the animal, insect and bacteriological kingdoms, the narrator's tone becomes gradually less respectful, more sardonic:

> Consider, with all reverence, the monkeys. May there not be a mansion for the monkeys also? Old Mr Graysford said No, but young Mr Sorley, who was advanced, said Yes; he saw no reason why monkeys should not have their collateral share of bliss, and he had sympathetic discussions about them with his Hindu friends.

The culmination of the enquiry is as brutally full of good sense as the rulers at the Club, and the narration mimics their voice:

> And oranges, cactuses, crystals and mud? and the bacteria inside Mr Sorley? No, no, this is going too far. We must exclude someone from our gathering, or we shall be left with nothing.

It is, however, only much later in the novel, at Mau, that it appears possible that these tones, for all their practical good sense, are themselves subject to contextual irony. Mr Sorley joins Mrs Moore and Ralph with Professor Godbole, possessors of some fundamental knowledge or instinct which renders Fielding and Miss Quested liable to seem as crass as the Collector.

The very success of Forster's presentation of the two latter demonstrates both the shortcomings of language as an instrument fit to enact religious revelation and of the development of a civilisation whose achievement is consonant with verbal expression. The unobtrusive confidence of the account of Aziz's encounter in the Maidan with the subaltern attends the presentation of the schoolmaster and the young woman. The reasoned good sense of the narration is wholly appropriate to these vintage liberal humanists. Like the narrator, Miss Quested understands clearly, if not at first her own limitations, at least those attendant on marriage to Heaslop and the British in India: "she would see India always as a frieze, never as a spirit, and she assumed that it was a spirit of which Mrs Moore had had a glimpse." This elusive "spirit" holds her interest, as it does the narrator's, and alienates her from her compatriots. Yet her charity and sympathy draw her back to them. In announcing to Heaslop that they are not to be married, her intellectual and morally scrupulous nature is infused with the flow of feeling:

> She felt ashamed. How decent he was! He might force his opin-ions down her throat, but did not press her to an "engagement," because he believed, like herself, in the sanctity of personal relationships.

> A wave of relief passed through them both, and then transformed itself into a wave of tenderness, and passed back. They were softened by their own honesty, and began to feel lonely and unwise.

The explicit metaphor is appropriate to the conceptions that Miss Quested and Heaslop entertain of themselves, in which personal relations, work, religious feeling and duty are readily understood as separate entities, and personality conceived in terms of "dryness" or "damp" does not nec-essarily appear ludicrous. Characteristically, the narrator, by drawing at-tention to the apparently irrelevant detail of the Indian bird that they see, disclaims their typical ordering of experience in this fashion, without in-sisting on its insufficiency. "Nothing in India is identifiable, the mere asking of a question causes it to disappear or to merge in something else": the comment reflects as much upon the genesis of *A Passage to India* as upon the characters it describes. Miss Quested's dissatisfied longing for a verbal absolute—" 'Mrs Moore, if one isn't absolutely honest, what is the use of existing?' "—is similarly pertinent to the novelist's sense of his vocation and the problems posed by the subject matter of India.

Fielding, while less naïve than Miss Quested, shares her limitations as well as her virtues. The latter include most obviously an attempt to ignore the racial barrier: "the world, he believed, is a globe of men who are trying to reach one another and can best do so by the help of good will plus culture and intelligence." Once again the aspiration's Schlegelian overtones reveal in how close a relationship this character stands to Forster's central preoc-cupations as a novelist, while the critique of his shortcomings shows the direction in which this novel develops by comparison with the rest of Forster's fiction.

Forster defined the humanist as possessing "four leading characteristics—curiosity, a free mind, belief in good taste, and belief in the human race," characteristics which Fielding shares. His humanism derives from personal conviction without philosophical or religious sanction. His disavowal of religious conviction scandalises his Moslem friends, but Forster admires the "zeal for honesty" that inspires his plain-speaking and his refusal to indulge in the easy, acceptable answers. Yet as the novel proceeds, Fielding's lack of spiritual development is shown as a disabling limitation. It accompanies a circumscription of spontaneous feeling similar to Miss Quested's: "he felt old. He wished that he too could be carried away on waves of emotion. Fielding's honesty has its price: "experience can do much, and all that he had learnt in England and Europe was an assistance to him, and helped him towards clarity, but clarity prevented him from experiencing something else." The virtues of clarity and honesty do not compensate for the fundamental commitment to instinct crucial to an understanding of Aziz, nor are they adequate to a concept as far beyond their range as the sense of evil:

> He felt that a mass of madness had arisen and tried to overwhelm them all; it had to be shoved back into its pit somehow, and he didn't know how to do it, because he did not understand madness: he had always gone about sensibly and quietly until a difficulty came right.

The metaphor of the pit dramatises the separation of conscious volition, which exercises the capacity for integrity and directness of address, from the unconscious, which prompts the entrapping of Aziz and the subsequent drama of Miss Quested's accusation and retraction: the latter demands response from a different source than that which regulates conduct, morality and justice. It is to Fielding's great credit (and a tribute to Forster's faith in the profundity of instincts for truth and decency) that he instinctively believes in Aziz, despite a personal philosophy which repudiates faith. The insistently spiritual context of the novel forces the realisation that this belief in Aziz is a quasi-religious affirmation:

> Fielding, too, had his anxieties . . . but he relegated them to the edge of his mind, and forbade them to infect its core. Aziz *was* innocent, and all action must be based on that, and the people who said he was guilty were wrong, and it was hopeless to try to propitiate them.

Yet despite the instinctive quality of Fielding's avowal, it rests on experience and the capacity to form workable judgments of people. Fielding's knowledge of his man is at stake, his sense of outrage located in the same area drawn upon by the novelist who offers an understanding of "character." Fielding's sense of limitation bears directly upon Forster's struggle with his art in *A Passage to India*. He reaches towards new understanding similar to that undertaken by the novelist, but unlike Forster it appears to elude him. At the moment of his great triumph over himself, when his dignified championship of Aziz withstands the insult of the Club's sneering disparagement, Fielding becomes aware of dimensions of experience foreign to his doggedly decent mentality. The Marabar Hills "leap into beauty," but the mythical associations (Monsalvat, Walhalla) conjured by the novelist do not touch the schoolmaster. Legal justice, due process of law, the bricks and mortar of civilisation occupy his interest: "who was the guide, and had he been found yet? What was the "echo" of which the girl complained? He did not know, but presently he would know. Great is information, and she shall prevail." Forster, by confronting justice with beauty, denies Fielding the enjoyment of his dignified triumph over pettiness and malice. While the latter has fought with great moral courage, it appears that he was entered in the wrong lists. His sense of discouragement derives not from the degrading spectacle of the British herding together under a banner that parodies his own, nor from the regrettable insult to Heaslop, but from an apprehension of inadequacy that short-circuits his usual channels of communication with himself. Justice, morality and decency at their best ignore too much of human aspiration and potential, and of forms of being that transcend the merely human. This central, beautifully controlled passage deserves full quotation:

> It was the last moment of the light, and as he gazed at the Marabar Hills they seemed to move graciously toward him like a queen, and their charm became the sky's. At the moment they vanished they were everywhere, the cool benediction of the night descended, the stars sparkled, and the whole universe was a hill. Lovely, exquisite moment—but passing the Englishman with averted face and on swift wings. He experienced nothing himself; it was as if someone had told him there was such a moment, and he was obliged to believe. And he felt dubious and discontented suddenly and wondered whether he was really and truly successful as a human being. After forty years' experience, he had learnt to manage his life and make the best of it on advanced

European lines, had developed his personality, explored his limitations, controlled his passions—and he had done it all without becoming either pedantic or worldly. A creditable achievement, but as the moment passed, he felt he ought to have been working at something else the whole time,—he didn't know at what, never would know, never could know, and that was why he felt sad.

The centre of experience appears to be mystical rather than ethical. Forster's prose contrives unemphatically the oppositions between the majesty of hills, starlight and universe, and the restrained evocation of Fielding's decency and self-dissatisfaction. The silence is felt, not remarked. The description indicates its presence in the phrase "lovely, exquisite moment" without allowing it to expand, because Fielding fills it with words directed inwards. Unlike Godbole later, he does not resist the impulse to conceptualise: the difference is stressed by the comparison "as if someone had *told* him." Silence, *A Passage to India* insists, must be felt. The superb, gently deflating phrase "wondered whether he was really and truly successful as a human being" rings achingly hollow in this context of physical beauty, mythology and eternity. Despite his concern for the oppressed, the wrongfully accused, despite even his awareness of his own circumscription, Fielding at such a moment is locked within the prison of the self. And despite her hostility towards him at this point in the novel, Miss Quested shares Fielding's nihilistic dissatisfaction, pointed by the quasi-religious context of her statement to Heaslop:

> "How can one repay when one has nothing to give? What is the use of personal relationships when everyone brings less and less to them? I feel we ought all to go back into the desert for centuries and try and get good. I want to begin at the beginning. All the things I thought I'd learnt are just a hindrance, they're not knowledge at all. I'm not fit for personal relationships."

By this recognition of their limitations, both Fielding and Miss Quested begin in some degree to "inhabit the desert," to withdraw from their compatriots and from intercourse itself into inner contemplative silence. But although they can go so far, they are incapable of greater self-transcendence. Miss Quested's resumption of her "morning kneel to Christianity . . . the shortest and easiest cut to the unseen" is the product of temporary distress rather than a sign of new understanding. She confesses wryly to Fielding her own sense of the shortcomings of honesty as a code, which parallels his own dissatisfaction. Immediately afterwards, however, they reassert their religious scepticism, explicitly disavowing any belief in an afterlife: "there was a moment's silence, such as often follows the triumph of rationalism." This silence differs qualitatively from that experienced and the consciously sought by Mrs Moore, Aziz, and Godbole. The sceptics' is, rather, a spiritual emptiness, the internal desert which clears the path to spiritual understanding but should never be confused with it. Hamidullah's lack of sympathy with Miss Quested after the trial examines the latter's valuable personal qualities in the light of a culture whose central emphases differ fundamentally:

> her behaviour rested on cold justice and honesty; she had felt, while she recanted, no passion of love for those whom she had wronged. Truth is not truth in that exacting land unless there go with it kindness and more kindness and kindness again, unless the Word that was with God also is God.

Miss Quested's triumph over herself by sticking to her principles in preference to not letting down her friends remains insufficient even judged from the standpoint of her own culture, as the culminating phrases of this description insinuate. Integrity and fairmindedness are shown to be just the rump of religion, admirable qualities indeed but spiritually speaking negligible. At the end of this scene at the College, when Miss Quested's lodging after the trial has been under consideration, Fielding in weariness is visited once again by the displacing vision of love crucial to Hamidullah's philosophy:

> fatigued by the merciless and enormous day, he lost his usual sane view of human intercourse, and felt that we exist not in ourselves, but in terms of each others' minds—a notion for which logic offers no support and which had attacked him only once before, the evening after the catastrophe, when from the verandah of the club he saw the fists and fingers of the Marabar swell until they included the whole night sky.

Once again the insufficiency of developing personality, exploring limitations and controlling passion as a goal of the whole man (rather than the civilised social being) has become apparent. Hamidullah's tone is taken up by the narration, when Fielding and Miss Quested offer their inadequate explanations of the experience in the cave and of Mrs Moore's intuitive understanding: "they had not the apparatus for judging." In condemning the inadequacy of their prose world, the narration adopts for purposes of judgment the idiom of Professor Godbole:

> When they agreed, "I want to go on living a bit," or, "I don't believe in God," the words were followed by a curious backwash as though the universe had displaced itself to fill up a tiny void, or as though they had seen their own gestures from an immense height—dwarfs talking, shaking hands and assuring each other that they stood on the same footing of insight . . . Not for them was an infinite goal behind the stars, and they never sought it.

At the end of the novel, Fielding's slightly regretful curiosity about Hindu religion confirms this Godbolian deployment of phrase, as he attempts to question Aziz about Ralph's and Stella's affinity (obviously transmitted by Mrs Moore) with Hinduism. Aziz is silent. The silence is entirely consonant with the subject that occasions it, as Mrs Moore has demonstrated earlier: " 'Say, say, say,' said the old lady bitterly. 'As if anything can be said! I have spent my life in saying or in listening to sayings: I have listened too much. It is time I was left in peace.' " The explicit attack upon language from Mrs Moore becomes vicious in its rejection of the novel's sole form of expression: " 'Oh, how tedious . . . trivial . . . ' . . . 'Was he in the cave and were you in the cave and on and on . . . and Unto us a Son is born, into us a Child is given.' " This develops more explicitly than the example cited earlier into a questioning of the idea of "character" as customarily understood by the novelist: " 'One knows people's characters, as you call them,' she retorted disdainfully, as if she really knew more than character but could not impart it." The "character" of Aziz only becomes available as we understand the silences of his religion and poetry. The narrator partly explains Mrs Moore's disillusion and feeling of displacement in the chapter which follows, but her own refusal to trust words is more significant as evidence to her capacity for in-dwelling, in such contrast to the eternally public world of the Club, and particularly of Fielding's and Miss Quested's best efforts.

The blend of sympathy and irony with which Aziz is presented illuminates the status of the latter tone in the novel. Irony in an important sense is equivalent to silence because it represents an implicit rather than externalised attitude to its subject. Yet irony is insufficient to Forster's purposes in presenting Aziz, who will increasingly command the narrator's sympathy as the novel progresses. In order to encompass the alien quality of this man's culture, Forster adopts a more tentative idiom than that used to portray the British: "Here was Islam, his own country, more than a

Faith, more than a battle-cry, more, much more . . . Islam, an attitude towards life both exquisite and durable, where his body and his thoughts found their home." Lionel Trilling remarks that "so far as the old Mediterranean deities of wise impulse and loving intelligence can go in India, Forster is at home; he thinks they can go far but not all the way, and a certain retraction of the intimacy of his style reflects his uncertainty. The acts of imagination by which Forster conveys the sense of the Indian gods are truly wonderful; they are nevertheless, the acts of imagination not of a master of the truth but of an intelligent neophyte, still baffled. However, it might be argued against this view that the narration's faltering into silence in the preceding quotation matches precisely the inarticulate nature of Aziz's own indefinite aspiration. Moreover, this willingness to trust to silence rather than more direct expression marks a primary strategy in Forster's attempt to penetrate eastern culture. The phrase "Islam, an attitude towards life both exquisite and durable" slackly generalises a sensation that exists in the blank space preceding it. Unless the reader links these words to the description of the mosque open to the moonlight, to the aspiration of Aziz which transcends patriotism, religion and valour, and then attempts to empathise with the silent crescendo of longing, the comment on Islam remains meaningless. In the description of the Bridge Party, for the most part incisively rendered in tones of English social comedy, the language again retreats from arenas to which speech is inappropriate. The contrast with the the prevailing idiom in that scene makes the insufficiency of verbalisation quite overt:

> There was a silence when he had finished speaking, on both sides of the court; at least, more ladies joined the English group, but their words seemed to die as soon as uttered. Some kites hovered overhead, impartial, over the kites passed the mass of a vulture, and with an impartiality exceeding all, the sky, not deeply coloured but translucent, poured light from its whole circumference. It seemed unlikely that the series stopped here. Beyond the sky must not there be something that overarches all the skies, more impartial even than they? Beyond which again . . .
> They spoke of *Cousin Kate*.

As the novel progresses, the distrust of verbalisation becomes absolute. Fielding refuses to point out to Aziz that water will not run uphill: "he had dulled his craving for verbal truth and cared chiefly for truth of mood." Mrs Moore refuses to accept her son's word's alone as an unimpeachable index of his state of mind and feeling: "his words without his voice might have impressed her." Her own invocation of the deity is subject to the same qualification: "She must needs pronounce his name frequently, as the greatest she knew, yet she had found it less efficacious. Outside the arch there seemed always an arch, beyond the remotest echo a silence." And this point of view is enlarged on at the caves in the reference to "poor little talkative Christianity." Nonetheless, Aziz's susceptibility to the poetry of religion fails to exempt his feelings from the strictures made by silence on words. Aziz's religion is scarcely closer to that reality than Fielding's ethical philosophy: " 'there is no God but God' doesn't carry us far through the complexities of matter and spirit; it is only a game with words, really, a religious pun, not a religious truth."

The clarity of Forster's probing analysis of the interaction between matter in the shape of language and the elusive spirit is a gauge of his own sensitivity to what his medium can, and, more importantly, cannot perform. The nagging uncertainty about the significance of the "echo" in the caves measures the novelist's refusal to accede to his form's propensity for continual explication. Only by attending to the breakdown of language accompanying the presentation of Godbole and the Hindu religion does the echo release its (strictly incomprehensible) "meaning." To begin with, Godbole refuses to "explain" the secret of the caves to Aziz and the English ladies: "the comparatively simple mind of the Mohammedan was encountering Ancient Night." Godbole preserves the enigma. Yet his singing transcends the petty temper which accompanies the ending of Fielding's tea party. The explanation of the song of the milkmaiden to Shri Krishna insinuates a possible reconciliation of eternity to time, by drawing futurity into the present:

> "But He comes in some other song, I Hope?" said Mrs Moore gently.
> "Oh no, he refuses to come," repeated Godbole, perhaps not understanding her question. "I say to Him, Come, come, come, come, come, come. He neglects to come."

Expectancy has been celebrated. This heralds the crucial understanding that the moment itself (rather than the structures of potential realisation and futurity built upon it), when prolonged, absorbs eternity. Significance resides in waiting. That is the condition on which insight and understanding become available.

Yet the point is not made explicit, because Godbole initiates his audience into participation rather than partial understanding. With the departure of the intrusive Heaslop the meaning of the song infuses the entire scene: "Ronny's steps had died away, and there was a moment of absolute silence. No ripple disturbed the water, no leaf stirred." Forster finishes the chapter on this (non)note of silence, prolonging its effect without attempting explanation. The words do not approach enactment but figure as signposts to a condition of feeling that is the antithesis of ratiocination, and therefore of language.

At the caves, Godbole's absence forms part of the atmosphere of doom that attends the expedition: "a new quality occurred, a spiritual silence which invaded more senses than the ear." Aziz's inadequacy to interpret the caves is related to the Hindu: "he had no notion how to treat this particular aspect of India; he was lost in it without Professor Godbole." Mrs Moore, shattered by the experience of the caves, can only respond to her feelings with direct honesty. She is unable to assimilate silence in Godbole's manner, to accept it fully. But she does register the totality of the silence and the apprehension of eternity:

> The echo began in some indescribable way to undermine her hold on life. Coming at a moment when she chanced to be fatigued, it had managed to murmur, "Pathos, piety, courage—they exist, but are identical, and so is filth. Everything exists, nothing has value." If one had spoken vileness in that place, or quoted lofty poetry, the comment would have been the same—"ou-boum." If one had spoken with the tongues of angels and pleaded for all the unhappiness and misunderstanding in the world, past, present, and to come, for all the misery men must undergo whatever their opinion and position, and however much they dodge or bluff—it would amount to the same. . . .
>   . . . suddenly, at the edge of her mind, Religion appeared, poor little talkative Christianity, and she knew that all its divine words from "Let there be Light" to "It is finished" only amounted to "boum." Then she was terrified over an area larger than usual; the universe, never comprehensible to her intellect, offered no repose to her soul, the mood of the last two months took definite form at last, and she realized that she didn't want to write to her children, didn't want to communicate with anyone, not even with God.

Where Mrs Moore approaches the obliteration of mental, spiritual and emotional distinctiveness that preludes the experience of totality or oneness, Godbole's culture, typically, enables him to make the necessary lesser distinctions between suffering and evil. His religious philosophy embodies acceptance, totality, reconciliation. His explanation to Fielding of Hindu concepts of good and evil strains Forster's prose style with its unwonted abstraction:

> "Good and evil are different, as their names imply. But, in my own humble opinion, they are both of them aspects of my Lord. He is present in the one, absent in the other, and the difference between presence and absence is great, as great as my feeble mind can grasp. Yet absence implies presence, absence is not non-existence, and we are therefore entitled to repeat, 'Come, come, come, come.' "

This difficult explanation of Hindu morality opposes Fielding's ethical philosophy, which remains determinedly secular. The certainty of Godbole's faith dissolves the sort of self-doubt to which Fielding is liable. Nevertheless, a noticeable feature of Godbole's explanation is Forster's satirical framing of it by Fielding's impatience, tiredness and boredom, and—to be anachronistic—the insistence on Godbole's Peter Sellers brand of near-fatuity and inconsequentiality. The result is not, of course, to deprecate the Hindu's faith, but the process of explanation itself. The enactment at Mau is accorded almost sacred respect.

To convey the intricate feeling of the Shri Krishna ceremonies, Forster stands his language on its head:

> Professor Narayan Godbole stands in the presence of God. God is not born yet—that will occur at midnight—but He has also been born centuries ago, nor can He ever be born, because He is the Lord of the Universe, who transcends human processes. He is, was not, is not, was. He and Professor Godbole stood at opposite ends of the same strip of carpet.

"Stands" in the course of three sentences becomes "stood." The change of tense indicates the co-presence of time and eternity. The antitheses "is, was not, is not, was," which further interfuse history and the present, are syntactically without meaning: Forster has exchanged the prose of reason and understanding for language as mystery, which modulates naturally into chant, " 'Tukaram,Tukaram.' " "Nonsense" becomes truth that lies beyond sense. Yet the language which is so effective at creating Fielding and Miss Quested is also capable of registering a range of feeling which is impossible to recreate more directly:

> When the villagers broke cordon for a glimpse of the silver image, a most beautiful and radiant expression came into their

faces, a beauty in which there was nothing personal, for it caused them all to resemble one another during the moment of its in dwelling, and only when it was withdrawn did they revert to individual clods.

The sign of divine presence and the language which records it are both inadequate to the state of feeling created by the ceremony, a failure transmitted again by Forster's ironic tones: "the God to be born was largely a silver image the size of a teaspoon." Yet his sign partakes, like the Cross, of the reality it represents, is, more properly, the symbol of "God Himself." Likewise, language transcends sign in the act of reading and becomes itself symbol, the chant:

> "Tukaram, Tukaram,
> Thou art my father and mother and everybody."

The necessary shortcomings of language, insisted upon throughout the novel, are transcended by the spirit of Hinduism which fleetingly gathers all mortal expression into a single communion: "God is Love." The fractured proclamation of Mrs Moore's hesitant insight much earlier in the novel, now repeated in a significant but unimportant abuse of language, heralds the spirit's attempt by "a desperate contortion to ravish the unknown."

Yet afterwards language once again must submit to its syntactical, hierarchical, time-ridden status:

> how, if there is such an event, can it be remembered afterwards? How can it be expressed in anything but itself? Not only from the unbeliever are mysteries hid, but the adept himself cannot retain them. He may think, if he chooses, that he has been with God, but as soon as he thinks it, it becomes history, and falls under the rules of time.

The clash of rowing-boats and the dialectical exchange between Fielding and Aziz prevent a simplistic reading of the closing Hindu sections as any kind of solution for problems of mortality, separation, racialism, or straightforward human cross-purposes. At the novel's end, the syntax recovers its confident tones confronting a reality to which it is fully adequate, and bangs shut like a gate: "no, not yet . . . no, not there."

Forster's language makes no pretense of dissolving the intractable difficulties it has created. Yet while it imposes its linear conception of time and its rational order upon the timeless, chaotic diversity of experience, language itself strives also to accommodate the twin sensations of flux and stasis. It forms a central communication with both aspects of our experience. Forster's language in *A Passage to India* possesses an essentially moral dimension—the only morality of art apart from the subject, as Conrad avowed—manifest in the scrupulosity it consistently displays towards its own status even as it shows a willingness to trust to experience beyond language. As such, rather than further perpetrate problems of inevitable alienation, Forster's stylistic delicacy recreates the complex interaction between certain individual, social and spiritual conditions of being in permanent but fluid form.

A Passage to India:
Forster's Narrative Vision

Barbara Rosecrance

In the final section of *A Passage to India,* Mrs. Moore reappears, again as an echo when Aziz hears her name in the interstices of the Krishna chant. Here the echo participates in a synthesis of all the earlier elements into a momentary vision of completion. Caves are included in the reconciliation, and the cycle in which they figured so destructively ends. Like the God, Mrs. Moore comes. As she seeks the God, Godbole comes to her. The earlier echoes that asked about divine presence are stilled in the momentary assurance of unity, and matter is comprehended in a transcendent vision of divine love. The Hindu celebration reaches a climax with the immersion of Fielding, Ralph and Stella Moore, and Aziz in the water of Mau's tank. The moment is accompanied by "an immense peal of thunder, unaccompanied by lightning, [that] cracked like a mallet on a dome." The "dome" recalls the overarching sky of the quest for an absolute, and the sound is significantly devoid of an echo. This is as final a suggestion as Forster makes, and it is tempered as always by the conditional: "That was the climax, as far as India admits of one."

Linked to the echo symbolism is the motif of appeal that voices the pervading desire for divine presence and seeks to bridge the prevailing chaos with hope of a divine order. Moving between the polarities of Mrs. Moore's nihilistic vision and the affirmation embodied in the Krishna ceremony, the appeals demonstrate above all that the prevailing condition of life on earth is contingency. Thus, of what use, Forster asks, are light, bell, or brake to a cyclist "in a land where the cyclist's only hope is to coast from face to

From *Forster's Narrative Vision.* © 1982 by Cornell University Press.

face, and just before he collides with each it vanishes?" The association of "only hope" with "land" suggests India's need. She entreats relief from her chaos: though practiced in an existence that depends on forces outside human will, her inhabitants have no control over their destinies. To a degree this is Forster's point, seen elsewhere, about the insecurity of life, but India is at once the context and symbol of a helplessness that has become the dominant characteristic of existence. Luck, not virtue, provides the only hope.

When early in the action Aziz stands by a mosque and contemplates "the complex appeal of the night," the array of smells and sounds that calls to him encompasses man and nature, East and West, life and death. The calls that resound through the novel usually bring no response. All versions of appeal have in common the elusiveness of the object. Thus Aziz tries to recall his dead wife, "not realizing that the very fact that we have loved the dead increases their unreality, and that the more passionately we invoke them the further they recede." More centrally, man's appeal to deity goes unanswered, as Godbole's song illustrates.

Godbole's entreaty at the tea party is premonitory: occasioned by the coalescence of caves and human muddle, the appeal to the absent God permeates the developing action. Godbole has announced that his song is "composed in a raga appropriate to the present hour, which is the evening." When, shortly, Ronny and Adela talk, Adela finds "no point in being disagreeable to him and formulating her complaints against his character at this hour of the day, which was the evening." Forster's language echoes Godbole's remark about the "appropriateness" of his appeal. The song has been followed by a moment of total silence, a moment of nothingness. Ronny and Adela are heavy in spirit, the sun is "declining," the trees hold a "premonition of night." Ronny and Adela's confused course, which will end in their misconceived engagement, is "appropriate" to a situation from which the god is absent.

When, moments later, Ronny and Adela ride without enthusiasm in the Nawab Bahadur's car, the theme of Godbole's raga reappears. The vast and inferior landscape mirrors the prevailing human inadequacy and similarly entreats divine presence; "In vain did each item in it call out, 'Come, come.' There was not enough god to go round." With the accident on the Marabar road that results in Ronny and Adela's spurious unity, Forster again invokes the language of Godbole's raga, reiterating the "appropriateness" of divine absence in such a circumstance: "Neither had foreseen such a consequence. She had meant to revert to her former condition of important and cultivated uncertainty, but it had passed out of her reach at its appropriate hour."

Appeals appear in comic variation, permeating the Indian environment. Thus, Ronny summons his servant:

> "Krishna!" Krishna was the peon who should have brought the files from his office. He had not turned up, and a terrific row ensued. . . . Servants, quite understanding, ran slowly in circles, carrying hurricane lamps. Krishna the earth, Krishna the stars replied, until the Englishman was appeased by their echoes.

Though the context appears trivial, Forster's symbols reiterate the major themes, and the incident itself follows the pattern of other appeals to the god. The servants run in circles—a recurring image that implies the search for completion, they carry lamps, which recall the stars of the opening chapter and imply a firmament that in fact appears in the next sentence. Ronny's calls echo outward to infinity, and like the god, the absent Krishna does not respond.

India is a land where masters can call and not call, servants hear and not hear, where everything is ambiguous, indefinable, constantly altering, and illusory or real, depending on one's perspective. In such a context, appeals reflect the prevailing conditionality. Aziz, beseiged by his friend Hamidullah's wife's insistence that he marry, responds, " 'Perhaps . . . but later . . .' his invariable reply to such an appeal."

Appeal figures in the familiar context of human invitations and rejections. The different church bells call respectively to Anglo-India and to mankind. To the Moslems, Godbole becomes tinged with political miasma when he seeks another Hindu as physician. "Everybody looked and felt shocked, but Professor Godbole had diminished his appeal by linking himself with a co-religionist. He moved them less than when he had appeared as a suffering individual. Before long they began to condemn him as a source of infection."

Art expresses the human need for divine reassurance. Aziz's recitation to his friends is such an appeal.

> The poem had done no "good" to anyone, but it was a passing reminder, a breath from the divine lips of beauty, a nightingale between two worlds of dust. Less explicit than the call to Krishna, it voiced our loneliness nevertheless, our isolation, our need for the Friend who never comes yet is not entirely disproved.

This passage moves to the heart of Forster's concern. The narrator combines a triple series of nouns, "loneliness," "isolation," and the culminating "need" with the concept of the deity: the "Friend," as Aziz elsewhere informs Fielding, is "a Persian expression for God." Again one is left with the overwhelming sense of the conditional: the only thing certain is uncertainty, yet this enables one to continue calling for the God.

Thus, aware that the God will remain absent, Godbole continues to entreat His presence. His serenity rests on two major premises. The first is that "nothing can be performed in isolation. All perform a good action, when one is performed, and when an evil action is performed, all perform it." Following from this, "When evil occurs, it expresses the whole of the universe. Similarly when good occurs." By such an account, all are implicated in the events of the Marabar, as the action itself demonstrates. The second tenet of Godbole's religious belief is expressed in his ability to distinguish between good and evil and yet to comprehend both.

> "Good and evil are different, as their names imply. But, in my own humble opinion, they are both of them aspects of my Lord. His is present in the one, absent in the other, and the difference between presence and absence is great, as great as my feeble mind can grasp. Yet absence implies presence, absence is not non-existence, and we are therefore entitled to repeat, 'Come, come, come.' "

Bridging absence and presence, the appeals continue. An appeal to Mrs. Moore presents a muted and ironic counterpoint to Aziz's trial. The British are responsible for her invocation, an action that contravenes their own interest in convicting Aziz. Mrs. Moore as Hindu goddess is a not inappropriate "travesty," because she has been closest of any western character to the Hindu identification of divine love with all matter. Mrs. Moore herself cannot come, not only because she is on a ship bound for England, but because she is dead, a fact known only to Forster, who withholds it here from characters and reader alike. Now summoned by the Indian populace, she "comes" to rescue her friend. The powers of love and truth have prevented a travesty of justice.

But Esmiss Esmoor cannot prevent the effects of the residue of the Marabar—a near riot at the Minto hospital, in which "the spirit of evil again strode abroad," continuation of a supercilious English officialism, and most important, the disintegration of the friendship between Aziz and Fielding. Ironic and thwarted appeals accompany the process. Forster places his characters in the position of the God, a role they are unable to assume—illustrating once again the human separation from meaning. Meeting Adela after the trial, Hamidullah is cold, even cruel to her, and Forster explains that if Adela had appealed to him, had "shown emotion in court, broke down, beat her breast, and invoked the name of God . . . ," Hamidullah would perhaps have placed himself in the position of the Divinity, for "she would have summoned forth his imagination and generosity—he had plenty of both." When Ronny arrives, Hamidullah's sardonic exclamation, "He comes, he comes, he comes," repeats the religious summons. Fielding influences Aziz to let Adela off paying compensation money by appealing to the memory of Mrs. Moore, a deliberate manipulation that produces the desired result but also furthers Aziz's suspicion that Fielding wants to marry Adela himself.

The appeals that sound through the novel culminate in the Temple section, where without deliberation or volition—and part of Forster's message is that man cannot will his own salvation—Godbole sees the entreating image of Mrs. Moore. She "happened to occur among the throng of soliciting images, a tiny splinter." Transcending in his religious ecstasy the limitations of his daily humanity, Godbole answers the appeal. His response both echoes and completes his earlier explanation of the legitimacy of appeal.

> He was a Brahman, she Christian, but it made no difference, it made no difference whether she was a trick of his memory or a telepathic appeal. It was his duty, as it was his desire, to place himself in the position of the God and to love her, and to place himself in her position and to say to the God, "Come, come, come."

It has already been noted that although Godbole includes in his love both Mrs. Moore and a wasp she had previously blessed, his human limits balk at the stone on which the wasp is seated. But that his act implies some measure of resolution, the repeated associations and images suggest, the action demonstrates, and Forster's comments on the genuine if evanescent unity achieved by the Krishna festival, imply.

Thus, where the original wasp "clung" to a peg, Mrs. Moore has "round her clinging forms of trouble." Reiterated and amplified, the original association finds embodiment in the action. Ralph Moore and Aziz meet as Ralph is stung by bees. Their relationship begins with trouble, for Aziz is hostile and cruel; but Ralph's challenging directness, similar to his mother's insight, allows the cycle that began at the Chandrapore mosque to find completion in the meaning of the temple at Mau, to which Ralph himself becomes, as Aziz recognizes, a "guide." For the characters, the Marabar is wiped out in the mutual understanding of Aziz and Ralph and the renewed though valedictory friendship of Fielding and Aziz. In the jubilation of the Hindu festival, the Marabar is drowned, and the actual immersion of Aziz, Fielding, and the younger Moores in the Mau tank marks the disorganized culmination of an affirmed unity that can exist only in the paradox of its temporary nature, and can be expressed only in itself. Of the moment of Krishna's birth that unites all matter in a vision of divine love, Foster says: "not only from the unbeliever are mysteries hid, but the adept himself cannot retain them. He may think, if he chooses, that he has been with God, but, as soon as he thinks it, it becomes history, and falls under the rules of time." Finally, in the symbolic sacrifice of the God himself, the counterpart of Godbole's abnegation of personality to achieve a limited version of divine love, Forster describes the unity that is both real and inaccessible:

> Thus was He thrown year after year, and were others thrown—
> little images of Ganpati, baskets of ten-day corn, tiny tazias after
> Mohurram—scapegoats, husks, emblems of passage; a passage
> not easy, not now, not here, not to be apprehended except when
> it is unattainable: the God to be thrown was an emblem of that.

The paradoxical, ungraspable nature of this vision returns us once more to the idea of conditionality. Like the reiterations of appeal, but with a more restricted focus, Forster's rhythmic uses of the word "perhaps" render the dominance of contingency. In the deliberate ambiguities of "perhaps," Forster implies a multiple sense of possibility, the simultaneous existence of a complex array of motives or factors, the difficulty of rational comprehension of the universe, and the limitations of man's ability to achieve earthly unity or comprehend a divine one.

Many of the contexts in which "perhaps" occurs are comic and apparently trivial. But the associations invariably have deeper connections. Forster tells us, for example, that Mrs. Moore's famous wasp "perhaps" thought the peg he had occupied was a branch, because "no Indian animal has any sense of an interior." Animals do not differentiate man's order from theirs: to them he is just another creature, and his distinctions are irrelevant to the natural world. "Perhaps" in this context serves the theme of man's separations and exclusions which contrast with the lower animals' instinctive perception of unity, an awareness that in her loving benediction, Mrs. Moore shares. "Perhaps" is again associated with man's exclusions when Forster comments, "All invitations must proceed from heaven perhaps; perhaps it is futile for men to initiate their own unity." Here the conditional mitigates the finality of a statement that would otherwise have the effect of a verdict.

As we have elsewhere seen, truth in India is elusive, conditional, and largely unknowable. The Russell's viper that appeared in the Government College classroom of an unpopular master "perhaps" "had crawled in of itself, but perhaps it had not." At the trial, a comment about Adela's ugliness "fell from nowhere, from the ceiling, perhaps. . . . One of the native policemen took hold of a man who had said nothing, and turned him out roughly." One notes about this passage the ascendancy of truth of mood over truth of fact: ejecting someone from the courtroom satisfied the English need for decisiveness and identification, but the remark that fell from "nowhere" expresses a truth to which this kind of identification is irrelevant. More important is the coalescence, in this brief incident, of "nowhere," "perhaps," and "nothing," thus connecting the essential quality of the caves with the conditional and unknowable nature of truth.

The human capacity to envision a cosmic unity is partial: as noted earlier, this is the meaning of the "perhaps" that qualifies Forster's attribution of pain to stones. Forster's narrative voice is essential to these insights, for the characters can apprehend them far less than he. Thus the narrator is predominantly the source of "perhaps" in the novel. Whereas Fielding and Adela cannot even conceptualize the important questions, the narrator simultaneously passes judgment on their limited consciousnesses and voices the problem.

> Were there worlds beyond which they could never touch, or did all that is possible enter their consciousness? They could not tell. They only realized that their outlook was more or less similar, and found in this a satisfaction. Perhaps life is a mystery, not a muddle; they could not tell. Perhaps the hundred Indias which fuss and squabble so tiresomely are one, and the universe they mirror is one. They had not the apparatus for judging.

The conditional always recalls the limitations of human awareness and capacity. "Before birds, perhaps . . . ," the planet must have looked like the approach to the Marabar. The assurance that sounds in Forster's voice throughout the novel expresses his certainty that cosmic answers are not available to man. If "proportion" is to be found anywhere in *A Passage to India,* perhaps it is revealed in the way Forster balances between the powerful negation of the Marabar and the reconciling but transitory assertion of divine unity at Mau. Exemplifying this is a question that, although a whimsical inversion of Mrs. Moore's fragile faith, far transcends whimsy in its implications: "God si Love. Is this the final message of India?"

Forster's reflection on the Hindu inscription implies both its illustration of the prevailing contingency and the chaotic, topsy-turvy quality of the

Hindu forms, With this, we confront the question of Forster's attitude to Hinduism and his intentions regarding the character Godbole.

Godbole is able to comprehend metaphysical complexities that elude the other characters. His disquisition on good and evil provides the only direct clarification of the meaning of the caves. When Fielding, depressed and irritated, is "obliged to listen to a speech which lacked both basis and conclusion, and floated through air." Forster affirms Godbole's sagacity and depth: "no eye could see what lay at the bottom of the Brahman's mind, and yet he had a mind and heart too, and all his friends trusted him, without knowing why." Godbole's reasoned exposition is a refutation of Fielding's exasperated comment that "everything is anything and nothing something." At Godbole's first entrance, Forster has associated him with harmony, "as if he had reconciled the products of East and West, mental as well as physical, and could never be discomposed." Finally, and most important, it is Godbole who is granted the reconciling vision.

Yet there is much to show that Forster draws back from a full embrace of Hinduism. His treatment of Godbole is affectionate but detached. The old man changes the subject "in the same breath, as if to cancel any beauty his words might have contained." Godbole is as subject as any character to the indignities that beset human frailty, as Dr. Panna Lal's diagnosis amply demonstrates. Fielding's observation that for the Hindu tranquility swallows everything else is borne out in the details of Godbole's portrayal. He eats in apparent oblivion to everyone and everything, he misses the crucial train to the Marabar, he discourses obliquely and with evident triviality in the face of Aziz's crisis. Forster observes that only a tiny fragment of Professor Godbole attends to worldly matters at all, and the comic proof of this pudding is the conversion of the King George V Emperor School, Godbole's major project as newly appointed minister of education at Mau, to a granary.

It is true that such affirmation as exists occurs in the context of the Hindu metaphysic. But the gap between vision and achievement exists for all humanity, and the concept of unity is not presented as a solution translatable into action. Moreover, while Forster respects the inclusion of incongruity, merriment, joy, and vulgarity in the Hindu ritual, his development of its chaos and formlessness reveals his fundamental detachment. Forster notes that "this approaching triumph of India was a muddle (as we call it), a frustration of reason and form." He qualifies any notion of climax—"as far as India admits of one," and the festival sums up as a "great blur" of which no one can locate the "emotional centre." This does not vitiate the vision, but it separates Forster's narrative voice from participation in the Hindu aesthetic, even as he insists on the relativism of the western view—"as we call it." Forster's western orientation similarly dominates his apprehension of Godbole's song, which he can describe only in the categories of western music, to which it does not adhere: "The sounds continued and ceased after a few moments as casually as they had begun— apparently halfway through a bar, and upon the subdominant."

Stella Moore, who in her husband's words, is "after something," has discarded the Christianity her mother found wanting and likes Hinduism, but not its forms. In detailing the whimsy, the ineffectuality, and the form-less fluidity of both Hindu ritual and the major Hindu character, Forster distances himself from their limitations and withholds endorsement of Hinduism as institution and panacea even as he synthesizes and renders the Hindu vision in its fullest meaning. I cannot agree with James McConkey that Godbole is "the character-equivalent of the Forsterian voice," because Forster's voice so transcends Godbole in its comprehensive articulation of a conditional order in the universe and at the same time reduces Godbole, through his particular inadequacies, to the level of the other characters. Hinduism furnishes Forster with the metaphor of inclusiveness, but no system receives his unqualified endorsement.

Through the Hindu celebration at Mau, then, Forster makes explicit the conception of a divine unity that counters the message of the caves. The vision is Janus-faced: in an interview with Angus Wilson, Forster himself referred to Mrs. Moore's experience as "the vision with its back turned," and Alan Wilde records Forster as having called the Temple episode Mrs. Moore's vision "turned inside out." The caves reduce all diversity and distinction to a single dull sound and collapse the temporal and spatial categories by which human beings try to order their perceptions. Characterized by "nothing," the caves transform the impulses of the phenom-enological world in their image: "everything exists, nothing has value." To this apocalyptic insight Forster offers an opposing vision that both includes and transcends the nihilistic message of the caves by asserting essentially that "everything exists, everything has value." Thus the cata-logue of diverse elements—birds, railways, foreigners, stars, stones—for whom "all sorrow is annihilated"; thus also the necessary inclusion of the untouchable sweepers in the ceremony of salvation. Thus, finally, the in-sistence on "completeness, not reconstruction." Neither Mrs. Moore nor the wasp can be reconstructed, but they can be absorbed into a vision that signifies a near-universal (balking the stone) acceptance of all matter. Sim-ilarly, Fielding's well-intentioned attempt to "reconstruct" for Aziz the course of their misunderstanding has no relevance: it requires Ralph

Moore's intuitive responsiveness to restore amity and bring the cycle to completion.

The cyclical nature of *A Passage to India* appears in the progressions of Forster's expanding imagery, in the thematic and structural categories of mosque, caves, temple, and the Indian seasons that move from an illusory calm to the destructive hot weather to the regenerating rainy season. In its climaxes and returns the action too illustrates the cyclical movement. Stella and Ralph represent an extension and rebirth of Mrs. Moore; through their appearance, the Marabar is wiped out. The union of Stella and Fielding, and most important, Stella's pregnancy, prefigure a new cycle and suggest the continuity that validates Mrs. Moore's final perception of "the indestructible life of man and his changing faces." In the midst of despair, amid the human chaos that India mirrors so faithfully, Forster has asserted that although God is "the unattainable Friend," he is nevertheless "the neverwithdrawn suggestion that haunts our consciousness." The search for unity, finally, has achieved a momentary perception of divine order; evil is absorbed and transcended in a larger vision, the cycle has run its course.

Is *A Passage to India,* then, as Wilfred Stone believes, essentially a revelation of unity, a declaration of independence from earlier repressions, in which Forster displays "spiritual gusto" and immerses himself with "joy" in an orgy of "mud-bespattered hilarity"? Does Forster make less of the cleavages of men "than of the unity encircling them," less of the separations "than of the single context in which they exist"? Some critics would deny what Stone's view assumes, that the novel should be read in terms of its climatic moments, and that one mood dominates. But we may read the novel as process and at the same time identify a pervading intention.

For although Forster suggests the existence of ultimate meaning, his characters grapple with a condition that seems rather to deny meaning. Seen as a kind of coda to the prehistory that produced the Marabar, the human span is insignificant. Man's efforts have resulted merely in a cyclical succession of fruitless conquests. Such as they were, the glories of man's history are behind him. Aziz is a sentimental eulogizer, and the triumphs of Babur and Alamgir have descended into the pettiness of Anglo-Indian tensions and intra-Indian bickering. The English are only the last of a series "who also entered the country with intent to refashion it, but were in the end worked into its pattern and covered with its dust."

Politics is reduced to "quarrels" that are "the malaise of men who cannot find their way home." India is inaccessible to the amenities of a vanished ideal, Edwardian Cambridge, where "games, work, and pleasant society had interwoven, and appeared to be sufficient substructure for a national life." Personal relationships cannot bridge the prevailing political atmosphere of "wire-pulling and fear." The dilemma is paradoxical, for politics "ruin the character and career, yet nothing can be achieved without them." An end to imperialism will not engender Indian unity: relieved of the English, the Indians will only reacquire their chronic disunities. Hamidullah, "on his way to a worrying committee of notables, nationalist in tendency," knows that "if the English were to leave India the committee would vanish also." Personal relationships are similarly transitory. The affirmation of unity at Mau fades quickly to return us to the frustrations of human reality. On his final ride with Fielding, Aziz "paused, and the scenery, though it smiled, fell like a gravestone on any human hope. . . . The divisions of daily life were returning, the shrine had almost shut."

The vanity of human wishes seems matched by the smallness of the characters, and some critics have complained that Forster's characters are insufficient to his theme. But against the idea of India, vast in scale, complex in its fragmentation, helplessness, and potential unity, the human characters are necessarily small: indeed this is the point. All of them share in the general reduction, to all he presents a detachment laced with irony. The characterizations are nevertheless noteworthy for their diversity and individuality. Forster presents Ronny as arrogant but honest, small-minded but conscientious, human both in his irritation at an unfathomable and inconveniencing parent and in his attempt to see Adela through. The other Anglo-Indians are treated in less depth but with equal justice. Mr. Turton, for all his officialism, does not hate Indians. Forster comes close to approval of his courteous realism in managing the "Bridge Party"; yet the Collector is subject to the raging jingoism that besets English and Indians alike after the caves incident. McBryde, the police superintendent, is treated with sympathy as well as irony. He "was the most reflective and best educated of the Chandrapore officials. He had read and thought a good deal, and, owing to a somewhat unhappy marriage, had evolved a complete philosophy of life." But McBryde is salacious and cynical about Aziz, and Forster hoists him on his own petard by catching him in an illicit affair.

The portraits of the Indians are similarly diverse. Hamidullah, the Cambridge-educated lawyer, is sentimental about the British and intellectually closer to Fielding than is Aziz. The Nawab Bahadur, a copious mixture of superstition and shrewdness, political astuteness and verbose generosity, is a kind of counterpart to the Collector—more sympathetically treated, but aware, as is the English official, of the difficulties both sides must face. Ram Das, the beleaguered Hindu magistrate who presides at the trial, is a man of capacity and understanding. More straightforward and articulate than Aziz, he is a force for unity among Indians themselves. Indeed the only Indian character whose contempt for the English is invariable is the coarse and conniving Mahmoud Ali, whose jealousy and jingoism contribute to the estrangement of Aziz and Fielding.

In considering Forster's attitudes toward his important characters, we may ask to what degree Fielding represents Forster's voice in the novel. Forster clearly stands behind many of Fielding's perceptions and assessments. Intelligent and intuitive, Fielding is the best of western rationalists, blessed with the capacity for affection, yet remaining in the Forster tradition of equivocal heroes for whom the world is a plunge beyond the capacities of a humanistic philosophy to mediate. Fielding, moreover, combines the best sensitivities of his forebears with the toughness they so conspicuously lack. Free of Philip's pretension and fastidiousness, more hard-bitten and realistic than Rickie, Fielding has managed to function among the transplanted Sawstonites who are the Anglo-Indians of *A Passage to India* without losing his humanistic ideals, his sense of humor, and his emotional independence.

Yet in his treatment of Fielding, Forster reveals his authorial detachment and the character's limitations. Fielding's motto is "Great is information, and she shall prevail." With all his intelligence and sympathy, the Englishman cannot cope with events or phenomena that defy rational explanation and reasonable solution. As he looks across from the verandah of the club to the Marabar Hills, they transmit a vision of his incompleteness, as powerful as the one that beset James's Strether in *The Ambassadors:*

> the cool benediction of the night descended, the stars sparkled, and the whole universe was a hill. Lovely, exquisite moment— but passing the Englishman with averted face and on swift wings. He experienced nothing himself; it was as if someone had told him there was such a moment, and he was obliged to believe. And he felt dubious and discontented suddenly, and wondered whether he was really and truly successful as a human being. After forty years' experience, he had learned to manage his life and make the best of it on advanced European lines, had developed his personality, explored his limitations, controlled his passions—and he had done it all without becoming either pedantic or worldly. A creditable achievement, but as the moment passed he felt he ought to have been working at something else the whole time—he didn't know at what, never would know, never could know, and that was why he felt sad.

Fielding, so superior to Adela Quested in his intuitive capacities, is reduced to her footing when confronted with the irrational. Forster's final judgment, that they are "dwarfs talking, shaking hands," represents the chilling reduction of a character whose capacities, infinitely greater than those of his earlier versions, have become irrelevant to the contemporary condition. Forster's most important humanistic hero, Fielding embodies the "proportion" that represented moral success in *Howards End.* But his wisdom, maturity, goodwill, and affection avail little. They do not allow him fulfillment in personal relations; more significantly, they do not enable him even to perceive the metaphysical question that animates the novel.

Forster's position as the unique interpreter of metaphysical truths is not, of course, new. His moral and aesthetic distance from the objects of his creation, however, reaches an unprecedented height in *A Passage to India,* and this distance is significantly paralleled by the situation of the character closest to Forster's insight. The search for ultimate truth that began with Philip Herriton's pilgrimage across Italy toward salvation has led in *A Passage to India* to a vision whose agent, Godbole, is notably detached from worldly matters. That Godbole's antics are the object of his creator's comic irony reveals him as cast in the same framework of limitation as the other characters. Withdrawal does not solve the political and social problems that the efforts to create personal relationships have so conspicuously failed to assuage. Yet although the moment is temporary, Godbole participates in an experience of reconciliation whose meaning lies in its analogy to the transcendent unity of divine love. But more significant than the ephemerality of Godbole's vision is the condition of its attainment. The possibility of insight can exist only through abnegation of self, through denial of will, through withdrawal from personal engagement. The attempts at human connection which the action sought unsuccessfully to sustain have yielded in the end to the tranquil indifference of a character who has "never been known to tell anyone anything." Detachment is thus seen as necessary to the inclusive vision that provides the only suggestion of God's presence, the only redemption from the certain frustrations of human effort. Between the first novel and the last, Forster has moved from the celebration to the abandonment of personality. Whereas in the earlier novels he resisted asceticism and withdrawal, the spiritual exploration of *A Passage to India* ends uncomfortably with a vision that precludes achievement in the world of action, a unity whose condition is the withdrawal from human concerns.

The implications of this radical change in position inform the language of *A Passage to India.* Forster's prose retains the comic irony, the deft reversals, the catalogues, the balanced phrases, the logical discriminations, the juxtapositions of apparent incongruities that characterized his technique in the earlier novels. His narrative presence is equally pervasive. Nor is it less didactic: it is only less personal. The impersonality that characterizes Forster's authorial presence in his final novel manifests itself in two major ways. The first appears in the combination of his narrative voice with the technique of purposeful repetitions of key words, images, and ideas—Forster's use of "rhythm." The second is to be found in the qualities of Forster's voice itself, as it simultaneously projects and embodies his bleak vision of man.

Voice and theme coalesce in the evocation of setting, as Forster presides directly over the Indian environment that engenders all the relevant terms of symbolic reference. The language of narration provides the images whose symbolic meaning evolves throughout the novel: the speaker's voice and the images it controls are integrated into a single context. At the same time, the purposeful repetitions create a new and impersonal sense of process and structure, in which such words as "caves," "arch," "echo," and "appeal" transcend their immediate contexts to acquire with each reappearance an increased breadth of suggestion and symbolic resonance.

Rhythm also appears in the novel in the simpler sense of beat or meter, and here too Forster replaces an earlier narrative directness with a different kind of emphasis. Repetitions of twos and threes play continuously around the major themes. Such rhythms may derive directly from the narrator, as when, describing the caves, Forster twice remarks on the "nothing, nothing" that characterizes them. They appear in the narrator's personification of setting—examples of this are the "pomper, pomper, pomper" of the train that accompanies the travelers to the Marabar, and the "ponk ponk" of tropical birds. They pass between narrator and characters, as the observation about the need for "kindness, more kindness, and even after that more kindness" moves from Aziz to Fielding to Forster's own voice. And they emanate directly from characters, as Aziz's furious "Madam! Madam! Madam!" when he thinks Mrs. Moore has desecrated his mosque by wearing shoes, and Mrs. Turton's estimate of men as "weak, weak, weak." In all their variations, however, the double and triple rhythms project an instinctual energy that counterpoints and augments the subtler and more complex repetitions.

But Forster's own voice in *A Passage to India* provides the most salient expression of his change of vision, as, constantly manipulating the relationship between environment and the limited human animal, he develops a world of ennui, indifference, and limitation. The remote perspective that dwarfs all the characters and regards them as part of an anonymous and helpless humanity dramatically illustrates Forster's own detachment from the agonies or triumphs of human personality. Concomitantly his narrative voice withdraws from the display of personality. Gone are the geniality, the chattiness, the essayistic interventions, the confidential air that implied a personal relationship with the reader. *A Passage to India* contains but a single incident of direct address—and it is directed with chilling irony to the terrors of Mrs. Moore's experience: "Visions are supposed to entail profundity, but—wait till you get one, dear reader! The abyss also may be petty, the serpent of eternity made of maggots." Earlier Forster implied the reader's capacity for insight and generalization; he now identifies the reader with the limitations of his characters.

The somber and impersonal voice of *A Passage to India* speaks of uncertainty in secure accents. Trilling's view that Forster's voice in his final novel is faltering and less prominent is belied both by the extent of the narrative interventions and by the declarative quality of the narrator's language. Forster insists on the reality of alienation with unequivocal verbs. His relentless repetition of detail creates the chaotic diversity of the Indian universe. His concrete diction defines an indifferent natural environment of sounds, smells, filth, dust, kites, and corpses that intensifies the revelation of human helplessness.

Forster's narrative language, his detached tone and remote perspective, dominate the novel, and the view they project testifies to the artist's degree of withdrawal from the world he has created. The human scale approaches the vanishing point, as Mrs. Moore and Adela play cards, indifferent to the rest of humanity:

> The day generally . . . acquired as it receded a definite outline,
> as India itself might, could it be viewed from the moon. Presently
> the players went to bed, but not before other people had woken
> up elsewhere, people whose emotions they could not share, and
> whose existence they ignored.

Man's spiritual and biological vulnerabilities merge in what is perhaps Forster's most extreme statement of human limitation. Stupified by the heat, the "Chandrapore combatants" soon yield to sleep: "Those in the Civil Station kept watch a little, fearing an attack, but presently they too entered the world of dreams—that world in which a third of each man's life is spent, and which is thought by some pessimists to be a premonition of eternity." Awake, man engages in trivial and fruitless bickerings. Unconsciousness consumes a significant part of his existence: even alive, he is close to the nothingness of death. Most important, man's impotence implies

God's absence. In attributing his observation to "some pessimists," Forster intensifies his impersonality while maintaining the bleakness of his view.

As the illustrations above suggest, Forster's withdrawal is integral to his vision of man's situation. But his detachment has further implications. As in the case of Godbole, Forster's withdrawal is the condition for his insight. The remote voice of the final novel is the primary means to revelation. Forster as narrator implies the connectedness of matter: it is he who interprets the moment of Krishna's birth and the significance of "passage." Like his first hero, Philip, "nobody but himself would ever see round it now. And to see round it he was standing at an immense distance." Forster has demonstrated in *A Passage to India* what a little way goodwill, intuition, and human effort will go. He has also, if briefly, transcended the implications of his story to speak of completion. In a prophetic voice and from an immense distance, he has suggested the unity of matter in a vision of divine love.

But the prophetic voice that separates itself from limited humanity is incompatible with the circumscribing devotion to human efforts. That the perception of divine unity is not translatable into social or personal fulfillment, the chronicle of historical exhaustion and human impotence makes clear. The scope of Forster's vision depends ultimately on his detachment from human claims or solutions. And for this there is a price. Amid the near-perfection of its ordered language, the narrative voice of *A Passage to India* has acquired the human exhaustion it so eloquently describes. In its detachment from character and reader alike, in its remoteness from the near if not complete futility of human action, Forster's voice projects a certain deadness of tone. Gone are the chatty disquisitions of *Where Angels Fear to Tread,* the passionate inconsistencies of *The Longest Journey.* In their place is an evenness, a deliberation by which Forster embodies a rich and coherent structure whose meaning, like that of music, is integral with its process and reverberates beyond its final sounding. But with the loss of hope and enthusiasm, with the unrelenting portrayal of limitation, with, above all, the extremity of withdrawal, Forster's voice moves toward confrontation with the implications of his vision. As his perspective recedes to infinity, so, as events have verified, Forster the novelist reaches impasse.

Forster's Friends

Rustom Bharucha

It is a sad photograph that should have faded with time. Perhaps it should not have been taken in the first place. The camera catches the two figures in a blank moment, their faces stiff, their eyes wide and vacant. The men seem to belong together like a married couple, but there is a rift between them. Outwardly, they resemble men of property, utterly respectable: their hair parted neatly on the side, their moustaches trimmed. Yet it is not a club that they belong to but a universe—of oblivion, separation, and death. Almost as a sign, the photographer has left an enormous space above their heads, a nothingness that seeps into the gulf between the men.

Looking at the photograph many years after it was taken, Forster observed that he looked "starry-eyed" in it, "very odd indeed." Significantly, he tore up all the letters that he had written to his mother from Tesserete, Switzerland, where the photograph had been taken. It was a time he would rather forget, reminding him of a relationship that hadn't worked out. As he put it, the holiday in Tesserete was like "a honeymoon slightly off-colour." The man who lost interest in him, preferring to flirt with a waitress, was Syed Ross Masood, Forster's lifelong friend to whom *A Passage to India* was originally dedicated. He is the other figure in the photograph.

Otherness is what initially attracted Forster to Masood. This "oriental" was unlike anyone he had met. In the suburban milieu of Weybridge, where Forster lived with his mother, Masood must have appeared like a sultan from the *Arabian Nights*—an alluring, exotic figure, well over six feet tall,

From *Raritan: A Quarterly Review* 5, no. 4 (Spring 1986). © 1986 by *Raritan*.

regal in style, histrionic in manner, and very handsome. When he got bored with the Latin Forster attempted to teach him, he would pick up his tutor bodily and tickle him. When his fellow students at Oxford ragged him about using scent, he simply "wiped the floor with one of them in a wrestling match." Masood was everything Forster was not—physically, socially, and culturally—and it is perhaps for that very reason that Forster came under his spell. On New Year's Eve, 1910, he confessed his love in his diary:

> Let me keep clear from criticism and scheming. Let me think
> of you and not write. I love you, Syed Masood; love.

These lines illuminate Forster's style of thought. First, the individual utterance—"I love you, Syed Masood"—then a break, an intake of breath signified by a semicolon, and then the thought itself—"love." Rooted in a person, and yet anonymous, detached. On reading the details of Forster's love for Masood so intimately recorded by P. N. Furbank in his celebrated biography—an intimacy so natural that Forster himself seems to be speaking to us—one realizes how much turmoil there was within Forster not only because Masood did not reciprocate his love, but because their friendship itself was based on differing conceptions of love, enigmatic, and left unexplained. Forster loved Masood and Masood loved Forster, but not in the same way.

It is too easy to use the dichotomy of East and West to explain the incompatibility of love between Forster and Masood. For one thing, if Masood was an "oriental," a man of the East, he was also an unqualified wog. And like all wogs, he was and was not Indian. He was the grandson of Sir Syed Ahmed Khan, the great Muslim reformer, but he was also the devoted foster son of Theodore Morrison, the principal of the Muslim Anglo-Oriental College at Aligarh which resembled Eton in its early years. Masood's sentiments were eastern, but his education was almost entirely western. On the one hand, he was entranced by Urdu poetry, particularly by the verse of Ghalib and Hali, but he also played the banjo and read the French symbolists. He never found time to attend meetings of the India Society at Oxford, but he was invariably free for a game of tennis. So how "oriental" was Syed Masood?

It would seem that Masood played with oriental images, fully aware of their stereotypes. Never embarrassed to indulge in grandiloquence, he once said: "Ah, that I had lived 250 years ago when the oriental despotisms were in their prime!" Clearly, he lived before Wittfogel and Said had their say about orientalism, and at a time when the British could still be tolerated by educated Indians. Masood enjoyed his role as an "oriental" and frequently wrote to Forster in the epistolary style of a Scheherazade: "let it be known to thee that thy slave's house was this day brightened by the arrival of an epistle from thee—the source of all his happiness." Even in jest, it is ironic for Masood to speak of himself as the "slave" (and of Forster as his "master"), because it was he who dominated the friendship. In fact, Masood was possessive of all his friends, whose attention he commanded in a vehement way. Not surprisingly, by the time he graduated from Oxford, his only friends were Indian with the exception of Forster and another Englishman. It seems that Masood's English "friends" could no longer accept his despotic view of friendship.

Forster learned to accept it in time. But in the early years, he must have been confused by Masood's protestations of love, particularly when they were yearning and not in the least possessive. For instance, in a letter written to Forster eight months before they went to Tesserete, Masood writes:

> Dearest boy if you knew how much I loved you & how I long
> to be alone with you. . . . Let us get away from the conventional
> world & let us wander aimlessly if we can, like two pieces of
> wood on the ocean & perhaps we will understand life better. . . .
> I only wish that you & I could live together forever & though
> that is a selfish wish I feel sorry that it will not come to anything.
> Did you see the eclipse, how beautiful it was!

What was this? Rhapsodic "oriental" rhetoric or true sentiment? It would seem that Masood had the latter in mind because in a subsequent letter he tells Forster: "you are about the only Englishman in whom I have come across true sentiment & that, too, real sentiment even from the oriental point of view." He then urges Forster to cultivate a faculty that every "true and well bred oriental" possesses—*Tarass*. For Masood, *Tarass* is that capacity to enter the feelings of another and absorb the atmosphere of a place. The oriental senses are always ready "*to receive* & quivering to receive some impression."

If Forster had possessed or had been possessed by *Tarass,* he would have embraced Masood when they once parted company at the Gare du Nord in Paris. He would have understood why Masood was so "extraordinarily sad." When Forster defended his crisp English goodbye by saying that they would be meeting in three days, Masood wailed: "But we're *friends!*" A parting had to be lingered over for Masood, otherwise how could friendship be savored? What was the point of saying goodbye if there was no sentiment attached to it?

Not only are the signs of friendship different for Forster and Masood, but their acceptance of sentiment in relation to love is also at odds. For Masood, sentiment seems to be the grace of love, and in its excess of feeling, it becomes the raison d'etre of friendship. It is beautiful in itself and does not have to lead anywhere or prove anything. Like a verse by Ghalib whose sounds hang in the air, waiting to be received and then fading away, it becomes that moment of intimacy which true friends share. In contrast, it would seem that for Forster sentiment is merely an attribute of friendship. In itself there is no guarantee of intimacy. No wonder he felt compelled to clarify his relationship with Masood. When he eventually confessed his love, Masood merely said, "I know," and allowed the moment to pass. For Masood, the intimacy of their friendship lay in the exchange of sentiment itself, not in the physical act of love. Many years later, Forster was to understand this. There is that inexplicable moment in *A Passage to India* when Aziz quotes Ghalib, and Forster reflects:

> The poem had done no "good" to anyone, but it was a passing reminder, a breath from the divine lips of beauty, a nightingale between two worlds of dust. Less explicit than the call to Krishna, it voiced our loneliness nevertheless, our isolation, *our need for the Friend who never comes yet is not entirely disproved.*

As Masood knew, his friend Forster would find *Tarass* in his art.

It is actually quite amazing that Forster and Masood were able to share as much as they did because the world they belonged to had a very rigid conception of how men should behave with men, and more specifically, how white men should treat black men. Colonialism, one might say, did not approve of intimacy between the rulers and the ruled. Not only did familiarity breed contempt, it also undermined the fundamental premises of authority and separatism that characterized the colonial administrative system. This position is staunchly upheld by Turton, the prototype of the *burra sahib* in *A Passage to India,* who says, "I have never known anything but disaster result when English people and Indians attempt to be intimate socially, Intercourse—yes. Courtesy—by all means. Intimacy—never, never." The sexual racism of the British is even more conspicuous in McBryde who assumes that "the darker races are physically attracted by the fairer, not vice versa." The intimacy he envisions, of course, is between a man and a woman. What would he have thought—and this is merely a perverse hypothesis on my part—if Aziz had made sexual advances to Fielding (or vice versa)? It is more than likely that this "crime" would have outraged not only his sense of decency and morality, but his very idea of manhood—not only his own sense of being a man, but his absolute faith in the masculine identity of his culture.

An ethos of masculinity developed during the British Raj of India, first in England, and then later, through a process of imitation, within India itself. Whether a man was serving his country at home or abroad, he was required to be "manly"—aggressive, competitive, and in control of his emotions and duties. The Empire had no particular use for women or for the values associated with femininity. Homosexuals were tolerated only insofar as they remained discreet about their activities and functioned within the strict confines of marginal societies like Bloomsbury and Oxbridge. It was among select and "understanding" members of these societies that Forster circulated his homosexual novel *Maurice,* which he knew could not be published "until his death or England's." While Forster was to have a fairly active homosexual life in England, particularly after he returned from India, he was no doubt aware that he belonged to the silent minority, a secret society of the sensitive, whose sexual ambivalence was symptomatic of their innate resistance to the authoritarian and paternalistic rule of their government. Fundamentally, Forster was caught within a system that upheld norms of manhood that contradicted his own.

Even in India he could not entirely escape these established norms, because they had been adopted by Indian men as their only alternative to defeating the British at their own game. In psychoanalytic terms, Indians had begun to "identify with the aggressor." Elaborating on this phenomenon in his brilliant study *The Intimate Enemy,* Ashis Nandy situates the opposition between *purusatva* (the essence of masculinity) with *klibatva* (the essence of hermaphroditism) as the essential conflict in the colonial psychology of Indians. "Femininity-in-masculinity," he claims, "was perceived as the final negation of a man's political identity, a pathology more dangerous than femininity itself." In reaction to this "pathology," there was an upsurge of "manly" sentiments and attitudes, martial acts of defiance, and frequently humiliating attempts to emulate the "tough politics" of the British. In *A Passage to India,* Ronnie speaks derisively of this nascent masculinity among the Indians, which his own government has unconsciously enforced. "They used to cringe," he says, "but the younger generation believe in a show of manly independence. . . . Whether the native swaggers or cringes, there's always something behind every remark, and if nothing else he's trying to increase his *izzat*—in plain Anglo-Saxon, to score."

The kind of "native" who asserted his masculinity was more often than not semi-Westernized. Masood, of course, was so Westernized that "manliness" was second nature to him. There is the famous story of his abrasive encounter with a British officer who ordered him out of a railway compartment. With his legs stretched out, Masood coolly said, "D'you want your head knocked off?" whereupon he and the officer became "excellent friends." The anecdote reveals the kind of tolerance, even camaraderie, that could develop between Indian and English men, particularly if the former imitated the manners of manhood assumed by the latter.

The real antagonists of Indian men were not their sahibs but the memsahibs who formed a minuscule society of their own. Excluded from any kind of meaningful social activity, they increasingly saw themselves, as Nandy puts it, as "the sexual competitors of Indian men with whom their men had established an unconscious homoeroticized bonding." Though this "bonding" is suggestively, though not explicitly, explored in the relationship between Fielding and Aziz, there can be no doubt of Mrs. Turton's racist abhorrence of Indian men. "They ought to crawl from here to the caves on their hands and knees whenever an Englishwoman's in sight, they oughtn't to be spoken to, they ought to be spat at, they ought to be ground into the dust." Significantly, this invective is aimed primarily at the white men in the room, Mrs. Turton's men, whom she considers "weak, weak, weak."

What is so astonishing about *A Passage to India* is that it resonates with these colonial attitudes and tensions while remaining a novel "set out of time." Forster scrupulously avoids specifying dates, though the imaginative space of the novel suggests an India that has passed through the Swadeshi Andolan and the Partition in Bengal. Now there is a deceptive calm, a scarcely controlled tension that threatens to break out into a national uprising. The novel is set within this tension and maintains a precarious equilibrium. Certainly, when Forster visited India for the first time in 1912, he became fully aware of the resistance to British rule, particularly through his meeting with two radical Muslim leaders, the brothers Shaukat and Mohammed Ali. Joint editors of an anti-imperialist journal, the *Comrade,* they condemned the British endorsement of Italian rule in Tripoli and supported the pro-Turkish movement among Indian Muslims. It is possible to see traces of this radical fervor in the "manly" Indian characters of *A Passage to India,* particularly in Aziz after the trial, when he becomes "an Indian at last." But Aziz's resistance to the British is deeply confused not only because he is a Muslim before he is an Indian, but because he doesn't know how to get rid of the British. All he has is rhetoric, emotion, and manliness. His cheers at the end of the novel, "Hurrah for India! Hurrah! Hurrah!" are like the echoes of the Empire mocking him.

And Aziz in an awful rage danced this way and that, not knowing what to do, and cried: "Down with the English anyhow. That's certain. Clear out, you fellows, double quick, I say. We may hate one another, but we hate you most. If I don't make you go, Ahmed will, Karim will, if it's fifty or five hundred years we shall get rid of you, yes, we shall drive every blasted Englishman into the sea."

Clearly, the novel was written before Gandhi's advocacy of nonviolence had acquired a national dimension. He needed less than fifty years not to "drive every blasted Englishman into the sea," but to convince them that it was time that they left. He alone knew how to deal with the manliness of the Turtons and the Burtons, not to mention Sir Winston Churchill. With his deceptively childlike and gentle manner, he strategically debunked the ethos of *purusatva* not to capitulate to the British, but to defeat them with another concept of manhood that brought the feminine instincts of man to the surface. As Ashis Nandy so accurately perceives, "Gandhi was clear in his mind that activism and courage could be liberated from aggressiveness and recognized as perfectly compatible with womanhood, particularly maternity." Though this alternative to the Western concept of manhood is something that Aziz has yet to learn, there is a moment in the novel when he does assert his manhood, not in Gandhian terms, but in the deeply personal tone of his author. It occurs when Hamidullah is talking to him man-to-man about "sticking to the profession" and earning the respect of European doctors. Aziz listens to the spiel, then winks and says, "There are many ways of being a man: mine is to express what is deepest in my heart." This is my moment of *Tarass* in the novel.

In *A Passage to India,* Forster attempted to express what was deepest in his heart. The writing of the novel was not easy. It wasn't just the incompatibility between East and West that proved to be an obstacle; Forster had reconciled himself to the fact that "most Indians, like most English people, are shits, and I am not interested whether they sympathize with one another or not." The novel was hard to write for personal rather than political reasons: it followed the death of a friend, another Muslim, Mohammed-el-Adl.

They had met in Alexandria in 1916 when Forster worked for the Red Cross and Mohammed was employed as a tram conductor. Not only was Mohammed Forster's first true lover, he was also the first man who challenged Forster to cross " a big racial and social gulf." He was Egyptian, a race more despised by the British than the Indians, and he belonged to the working class. He had more reason to be anti-British than Masood, particularly when in 1920, at the height of British colonialism in Egypt, he was sentenced to six months' hard labor in prison on a false charge of attempting to buy firearms. "They shaved the hair they used a filthy basket instead of a towel, took off my civil clothes and gave me a prisoner's clothes," he wrote incoherently to Forster who was "wrecked" by the news. The political forces of his country had humiliated his friend. There is some reason, I believe, for Forster to have written the notorious statement many years later in *What I Believe*: "If I had to choose between betraying my country and betraying my friend I hope I should have the guts to betray my country."

On returning from his second visit to India in 1922, Forster stopped over in Port Said to spend a few days with Mohammed, who was dying of consumption. He arranged for his friend to live in a health resort, bought a silk shawl for his wife, and made provisions for the family. This extension of friendship to the family of his friend is typical of Forster's later relationships with men. Mohammed's world mattered to Forster as much as did Mohammed himself. On returning to England, Forster simply waited for his friend to die. In his diary, he confided: "I want him to tell me that he is dead, and so set me free to make an image of him."

Mohammed died within four months, bequeathed a ring to Forster, and *A Passage to India* was well under way. If this sounds somewhat ruthless, an exploitation of life in the pursuit of art, it should be remembered that Forster also wrote a private "letter" to Mohammed after his death that contains some of the most poignant autobiographical writing that I have ever read. Through recollections of dreams and a confrontation of the struggle involved in making a dead person live, Forster forged his way to an acceptance of his friend's death in the larger context of being alive in the universe.

In the spring of 1923, he went for a walk in Chertsey Meads, wearing Mohammed's ring, and found that he could no longer remember his friend. He acknowledged the sad truth of this experience in his diary, and in the process of recording it, he crystallized his vision of friendship.

> You are dead, Mohammed, and Morgan is alive, and thinks more about himself and less of you every word he writes. You called out my name at Beebit el Hagar station after we had seen that ruined temple. . . . It was dark and I heard an Egyptian shouting who had lost his friend: Margan, Margan—you calling

me and I felt we belonged to each other, you had made me an
Egyptian. When I call you on the downs now, I cannot make
you alive, nor can I belong to you because you own nothing. I
shall not belong to you when I die—only be like you.

There is no otherness in this friendship. The categories of "you" and "me"
are dissolved; Forster can be Egyptian. Or more precisely, he can be made
Egyptian by his friend. Ultimately, these national distinctions are of no
consequence because in death, there is nothing to own—neither a name nor
a country. Even friends no longer belong to each other: they *are* each other.

This magnanimous view of friendship had evolved over time. Certainly, it would be wrong to assume that Forster had always upheld it or
had been guided by it in his attitude to men. During his second trip to
India, for instance, we have a document of his relationship with an Indian
boy called Kanaya that disturbingly reflects an authoritarian view of friendship based on the principle of ownership. Forster had met "this barber-
boy" while serving as the secretary to the Maharaja of Dewas Senior.
Unable to control his homosexual instincts ("the heat provoked me sexually") and oppressed by his constant masturbation and vacancy of mind,
Forster eventually found comfort in Kanaya, whose services were arranged
by none other than the Maharaja himself. While officially an "anti-sodom-
ite" (unlike the Maharaja of Chatrapur whose attachment to boy-actors
was well known), the Maharaja of Dewas sympathized with Forster's
problem.

"Why a man and not a woman?" he once asked. "Is not a
woman more natural?"

"Not in my case," replied Forster. "I have no feeling for
women."

"Oh, but then that alters everything. You are not to blame."

Not only was the Maharaja Forster's active accomplice in his sex life, he
even advised Forster to accept homosexual jokes made at his expense and,
at all costs, to avoid passivity, "for a rumour of that kind would be bad."
In a more tantalizing way, he revealed Forster's age to his courtiers under
the dubious assumption that "at forty-two any properly constructed Indian
is impotent or nearly so and can dally no more with maiden or boy."

While the Maharaja appears to us, quite literally, as a character—he is
whimsical and delightfully absurd in his maneuverings and strategies—one
should also keep in mind that he embodies power. As the ruler of the state,
he *owns* Kanaya's life. In his manuscript, Forster reveals that Kanaya was

"terrified of H. H., whose severity towards his class seemed notorious." And significantly, as His Highness's friend, Forster also assumes an ownership of Kanaya who has, in his words, "the body and soul of a slave." When Kanaya eventually attempts to exploit the relationship by endearing himself to the Maharaja, Forster reacts sharply:

> I hesitated not but boxed his ears. . . . He had been such a goose—had done himself and the rest of us in because he couldn't hold his tongue. What relationship beyond carnality could one establish with such people?

The petulance of Forster's tone and his very English dismissal of Kanaya as a "goose" indicate that he wrote his description of Kanaya to be read by or to friends in the Bloomsbury Memoir Club. It is for the amusement of these friends that Kanaya himself becomes a character, a source of entertainment.

Needless to say, one has no idea who Kanaya is apart from what we learn from Forster. Even his appearance implies ridicule: "Somewhat overdressed in too yellow a coat and too blue a turban, he rather suggested the part and his body was thin and effeminate and smelt of cheap scent." Kanaya hardly speaks, and when he does, he sounds as real as any slave in the *Arabian Nights* talking to his master. We have no way of knowing what he really felt and thought about being sexually involved with a sahib, because Forster does not permit him a point of view. It is possible that the value judgments made by Forster on Kanaya's behalf are a reaction to the "little racial vengeance" that he received from the local people in Dewas, who teased the sahib for liking boys. But there is no justification, I think, for the peremptory tone adopted by Forster in the conclusion of the piece:

> I resumed sexual intercourse with him, but it was now mixed with the desire to inflict pain. It didn't hurt him to speak of, but it was bad for me, and new in me, my temperament not being that way. I've never had that desire with anyone else, before or after, and I wasn't trying to punish him—I knew his silly little soul was incurable. I just felt he was a slave, without rights, and I a despot whom no one could call to account.

Despite the self-criticism which actually hints of selfishness ("it didn't hurt him, it was bad for me"), this attitude is undeniably despotic. I cannot help wondering how Kanaya reacted to this change in attitude by Forster. What happened to Kanaya anyway? And who *was* he in the first place?

I see a very slight and ineffectual Indian beginning to speak, but then, absurdly, there is an image of Forster's barber-boy "skipping away through the sunshine holding up a canvas umbrella to protect his complexion."

The inherent problems in representing Kanaya are symptomatic of the contradictions faced by Flaubert when he represented the Egyptian courtesan Kuchuk Hanem as the prototype of Oriental womanhood. Kanaya's misrepresentation seems inconsequential in comparison, but it echoes what Edward Said has said about Kuchuk Hanem: "She never spoke of herself, she never represented her emotions, presence, or history. [Flaubert] spoke for and represented her." It seems that representation in itself poses an unavoidable paradox: on the one hand, we have reason to be concerned when we believe that something or someone has been misrepresented, and yet, can there be a true representation of anything? What is the truth in a representation? Is it an essence that has been faithfully reproduced in the representation? Or is it, less ambiguously, a point of view that you happen to share with the author?

It is well known that the representation of the Anglo-Indian characters in *A Passage to India* was strongly criticized by many Anglo-Indian readers as "unfair" and "inhuman." "Your Collector is impossible," wrote a retired Indian civilian of "thirty years' experience" (as opposed to Forster's "year-and-a-half"). "All the fuss about the bridge-party is hopelessly out of date," wrote another. Ultimately, as Forster was to acknowledge with daring candor, "I loathe the Anglo-Indians and should have been more honest to say so." But does the fact that he "loathes" the Anglo-Indians imply that he doesn't *know* them? I think not, but then I speak as an Indian. Turton is not a one-dimensional caricature for me: he represents a particular combination of pomposity and power that was known to exist in colonial India. In fact, we still have Turtons in India today, only now their skin is "coffee-colour" as opposed to "pinko-gray." The *burra sahib* mentality is not obsolete at all: it is a living presence in post-Independence India and can be traced to the behavior of company directors and bureaucrats. In fact, replicas of Turton can be found all over the world, notably in members of Margaret Thatcher's party and in immigration officials at Heathrow Airport.

If I seem to be arguing as an "oriental" here, it is because I know when I like or dislike certain people, not unlike Mrs. Moore and her author. "Sympathy is finite," as Forster once remarked. As for "fair-mindedness," it was to be commended as a "rare achievement" in art, but "how sterile in one's soul." What mattered to Forster most of all as a writer was what he called the *accent* in a work of art. "If I saw more of Anglo-India at work," he explained to a critical reader, "I should of course realize its difficulties and loyalties better and write about it from within. Well and good, but you forget the price to be paid: I should begin to write about Indians from without. My statements about them would be the same, but the accent would have altered." It seems that the "accent" involves a great deal more than a change in emphasis of tone or point of view. In the case of Forster's depiction of the Indian characters in *A Passage to India,* notably Aziz, it becomes a sympathetic link that an author feels for a particular character that transcends the objectivity of his representation. The author may criticize this character, but fundamentally, he is linked to him rather like a friend.

One could say that Forster wrote *A Passage to India* as an "oriental," which in the context of the book signifies " a friend of the East." This does not mean, of course, that he wrote the book as an Indian. How could he? Like any author, his sympathies were circumscribed by his intellectual milieu, his personal and political commitments, and his sense of history—all of which had been unavoidably shaped by his English upbringing, education, and cultural inheritance. Obviously, the truth to be found in Forster's novel is something that has been shaped by Forster himself. It is not a metaphysical essence of India that has simply been borrowed and absorbed into the book. Therefore, in asking the inevitable (and problematic) question, How true is the book to India? one should keep in mind that the truth represented in the book is itself a representation. In other words, we have to examine its, as Said advises in *Orientalism,* not in relation to "some great original," but more concretely through the book's style, figures of speech, and narrative devices. The very exteriority of a text is what constitutes its truth.

Upholding this critical premise, Said quotes the famous ending of *A Passage to India* (perhaps more famous now after its rendition in David Lean's film) and comments that it is *this style* that "the Orient will always come up against."

> But the horses didn't want it—they swerved apart; the earth didn't want it, sending up rocks through which riders must pass single-file; the temples, the tank, the jail, the palace, the birds, the carrion, the Guest House, that came into view as they issued from the gap and saw Mau beneath: they didn't want it, they said in their hundred voices, "No, not yet," and the sky said, "No, not there."

It is almost as if Forster's language is setting up a barrier which prevents the East and West from coming together. Otherness seems to be affirmed through the rhetoric itself. One is left, in Said's words, with "a sense of the pathetic distance still separating 'us' from an Orient destined to bear its foreignness as a mark of its permanent estrangement from the West."

My problem with this interpretation is that it is much too strategic in its focus and situation in the wider spectrum of Orientalist thought. Yes, there is separation in the final moments of *A Passage to India,* but it is so subtly juxtaposed with intimacy that one might say that Aziz and Fielding have acquired a mutual understanding of each other for the first time— perhaps because of the separation. Let us not forget that before the horses "swerve" apart, the language is steeped in a physical detail that totally contradicts the "distant" style of the conclusion. Aziz is shouting,

> "We shall drive every blasted Englishman into the sea, and then"—he rode against him [Fielding] furiously—"and then," he concluded, half kissing him, "you and I shall be friends."
>
> "Why can't we be friends now?" said the other, holding him affectionately. "It's what I want. It's what you want."

The irony that Forster suggests so seductively is that Aziz and Fielding *are* friends at the moment of parting. If history and the universe are bent on separating them, Forster seems to imply that it is "not yet" time for them to be permanently united.

For me, the ending is not "disappointing" as Said claims. If Aziz and Fielding had galloped away into the sunset, it would have been as unconvincing as their gentlemanly handshake in Lean's film. Forster, I believe, is attempting something a great deal more complex than an orientalist vision of irreconcilable differences between East and West. One could say that he is juxtaposing three kinds of friendship: the friendship between friends, between nations, and between friends and (their friends') nations. The struggle between these different kinds of friendship is most richly textured in the final exchange between Aziz and Ralph. As Mrs. Moore's son, Ralph has to be Aziz's friend:

> "But you are Heaslop's brother also, and alas, the two nations cannot be friends."
>
> "I know. Not yet."
>
> "Did your mother speak to you about me?"
>
> "Yes." And with a swerve of voice and body that Aziz did not follow he added: "In her letters, in her letters. She loved you."
>
> "Yes, your mother was my best friend in all the world."

Truly, it is in language that the ambivalent truths of books are ultimately conveyed. In the passage quoted above, we find so many of the tussles within Forster's characters—their allegiance to themselves, to their friends, and to their nations—all cohering in an irresolute conflict. It is the words that carry this irresolution through to the end of the novel. It is "not yet" time for the nations to be friends. But more subtly, in Ralph's "*swerve* of voice and body," I sense a movement *toward* Aziz and the very counterpoint of the final separation between Aziz and Fielding when the horses swerved apart. In the separation, I hear an echo of the earlier movement.

Separating and uniting, giving and receiving, the novel moves between these states of being. The possibilities of friendship that lie at the very core of Forster's vision may be questioned, but they are not absolutely denied. As Ralph instinctively knows, even a stranger can be a friend. He is white and, in a sense, unavoidably related to the Turtons and Burtons (on a racial level) and to Ronnie (through his mother's first marriage), but he can also be an "oriental." And not through manipulative or exploitative means but by feeling something extraordinary about India of which Aziz himself is unaware. Stella also feels "that link outside either participant that is necessary to every relationship"—a link that she discovers after experiencing the Hindu celebration of Krishna. Forster poses here a controversial paradox in making Mrs. Moore's children seem more "oriental" than Aziz through their insight into Hinduism. As a Muslim whose allegiance is to Babur and Alamgir, the poetry of Ghalib, and the spirit of Islam, which is "more than a faith" for him, Aziz seems excluded from India in a significant way. While he is an "oriental" by birth (though he has no "natural affection" for his motherland), Ralph and Stella feel connnected to their colony on a spiritual level. Forster may be criticized for mystifying the "link" felt by the Moores, but it is gratifying that he does not uphold the orientalist dichotomy of "them" and "us" in a rigid way.

This does not mean, of course, that all westerners can be "orientals." Good old Fielding remains committed to his "Mediterranean norm." As for the other Anglo-Indian characters, they are orientalists by profession for the most part and are in India "to do justice and keep the peace." Their necessary commitment to recording, controlling, administering, and defining the Orient in their own terms is what prevents and forbids them from being "oriental." Forster's dislike of these orientalists is what prevents him from celebrating the "marriage" of East and West that Walt Whitman affirmed in his own *"Passage to India."* Written to memorialize the opening of the Suez Canal in 1869, the poem has nothing in common with the novel but the title. In fact, it seems that Forster has quite deliberately debunked almost every ideal rhetoricized in the poem.

The "doubts to be solv'd" and "blanks to be filled" mentioned in Whitman's poem are neither solved nor filled in the novel. "Old occult Brahma" becomes nothing and "reason's early birth" seems the very antithesis of the "muddles" that Forster's India seems to generate. The "great achievements of the present" which Whitman glorifies are conspicuous by their absence in Forster's world. Technology cannot explain the echoes in the Marabar caves. Ultimately, what Forster refutes in Whitman's vision of "the marriage of continents, climates, and oceans" is its assumptions of global order and universal brotherhood. The poem reeks of belief, an abstraction odious to Forster. All he really believed in, as he mentioned in a famous essay, was personal relationships. It is not surprising, therefore, that he did not share the grandiose vision of man symbolized in the building of the Suez Canal.

This ambitious project was unanimously heralded as a revolutionary step in uniting the peoples and nations of the world. "Now we will be one" is what Ferdinand de Lesseps must have envisioned. Not inappropriately, his investment company for the project was called the *Campagnie universelle*. "The whole earth" seemed to be involved in the project. On its completion, "this cold, impassive, voiceless earth," in Whitman's words, "would be completely justified." The truth, of course, is that it was the "engineers, architects, and machinists" from the West who "justified" the project. They were the initiators of this vision for the unification of the world. Their missionary zeal is very clearly reflected in a prize-winning poem on the Suez Canal written by Bornier. In the poem, it becomes clear that the Suez Canal has been created not only "pour l'univers," but "pour le Chinois perfide et l'Indien demi-nu." And inevitably, "Pour ceux à qui le Christ est encore inconnu." In such sentiments one realizes the racist dimension underlying global missions and projects.

A Passage to India does not share this global mission. The only oneness that is alluded to in the novel is one that an individual may find on coming to terms with Nothing. But apart from this uncertain tryst with the unknown, there are no solutions provided by Forster for the oneness of the world. Unlike de Lesseps, he would not, in all probability, believe that "le rapprochement de l'occident et de l'orient" could be achieved through building a canal. But perhaps, if a Brahmin schoolteacher with clocks on his socks remembered a wasp once observed by a white "oriental" lady—perhaps it was at such moments that the East and West could enter each other's minds. Now this preoccupation with wasps may seem precious to

Forster's critics, but even the severest among them would have to agree that there is nothing orientalist about it.

Minute in detail, it is symptomatic of Forster's distrust of big events—a distrust that challenged the pomp and ceremony of the Raj, its laws and proclamations, its edicts and messages. There is no colonial fervor in Forster to change India, no humanist scheme of progress imposed on a country ridden with problems. Forster accepted India for what it was, and therein lies the extraordinary strength and love of his novel. One can say that India was like so many of his friends. If he saw faults in them, they became part of his love for them. And as in any true friendship, his friends were "his for ever and he theirs for ever: he loved them so much that giving and receiving became one."

Forster's love for India endured and deepened over the years. It did not fade with time. When he finally returned to India in 1945 to attend a conference of writers, he again visited Hyderabad, Masood's home city, and realized "how much of his heart had gone into the place." Now he was a famous writer and Masood was dead. Seeking refuge from all the attention he received as a dignitary, Forster retreated to a hillside one evening and watched the sun set. Later, he revealed that he had been thinking of Egypt. In his memory, Egypt and India had coalesced, and his friends, too, Mohammed and Masood, were one. Forster never wrote about this moment. Perhaps he realized that some accounts of friends can be written only in the heart.

The Geography of *A Passage to India*

Sara Suleri

The adventure of twentieth-century narrative in English has engendered an area studies that, in the act of taking India as its subject, transforms the locality of an historic space into a vast introspective question mark. From *A Passage to India* on, "books about India" have been more accurately books about the representation of India, with each offering variants of the peculiar logic through which a failure of representation becomes transformed into a characteristically Indian failure. In order to examine such acts of representation as a mode of recolonization, I wish to present a reading of Forster's *A Passage to India,* a paradigmatic text of the subterranean desire to replay, in twentieth-century narrative, the increasingly distant history of nineteenth-century domination. The mode is characterized by the desire to contain the intangibilities of the East within a western lucidity, but this gesture of appropriation only partially conceals the obsessive fear that India's fictionality inevitably generates in the writing mind of the West. The symbolic violence of this fear underlies the impulse to empty the area out of history and to represent India as an amorphous state of mind that is only remembered in order for it to be forgotten.

From their titles on, narratives on the Indian theme declare their intentions to name something so vague as to be nearly unnameable, implying that their subject is disturbingly prone to spill into atmospherics rather than remaining fixed in the place to which it belongs. Something is dislocated, and the fictions proceed to develop on precisely those lines. Typically, the narrator is a cartographer, the only locus of rationality in an area of engulfing

---

unreliability, so that ultimately the narrative mind is the only safe terrain the texts provide. India itself, like a Cheshire cat, functions as a dislocated metaphor for an entity that is notoriously remiss in arriving at the appointed place at the correct time. As a consequence, it becomes a space that imposes its unreality on western discourse to the point where the narrative has no option but to redouble on itself, to internalize the symbolic landscape of India in order to make it human. Thus geography is subsumed into the more immediate and familiar territory of the liberal imagination, in the act of recolonizing its vagrant subject with the intricacies of a defined sensibility.

Such is the imagination, of course, that legitimizes a test like *A Passage to India* as a humanely liberal parable for imperialism, and allows a reader like Trilling to interpret the novel's depiction of Eastern action as a metaphor for the behavior of the West. In other words, the only difference of India inheres in the fact that it is symbolic of something the western mind must learn about itself. The paradigm that Forster establishes is of crucial importance to all subsequent narratives on India, which, with their exquisite caving in upon themselves, embody a response to the difference of India that Forster so effectively literalized. For it is Forster rather than Kipling who initiates the Western narrative of India: a text like *Kim* in fact reinforces the reality of India by seeing it so clearly as the other that the imperial West must know and dominate. *A Passage to India,* on the other hand, represents India as a metaphor of something other than itself, as a certain metaphysical posture that translates into an image of profound unreality. It thus becomes that archetypal novel of modernity that co-opts the space reserved for India in the Western literary imagination, so that all subsequent novels on the Indian theme appear secretly obsessed with the desire to describe exactly what transpired in the Marabar caves.

"How does one interpret another culture," asks Edward Said [in *Covering Islam*], "unless prior circumstances have made that culture available for interpretation in the first place?" This question, that of the historic availability of India, is certainly not a problem that preoccupies Forster's protagonists, who are far more interested in decoding that which India tells them about their own interpretability. Thus Forster initiates a narrative mode that is perhaps more fraught with violence than the Orientalist code that Said charts, which is that "imaginative yet drastically polarized geography dividing the world into two unequal parts, the larger, 'different' one called the Orient, the other, also known as 'our' world, called the Occident." Where Forster transgresses even an Orientalist decorum is by implying that India is really not other at all, but merely a mode or passageway to endorse the infinite variety that constitutes a reading of the

West. To approach the Indian fictions of the modern West is indeed to confront a secret attack on difference, and to reread the text that is *A Passage to India*. For this fiction most clearly delineates the desire to convert unreadability into unreality, and difference into an image of the writing mind's perception of its own ineffability.

Forster, I hope to demonstrate, constructs a symbolic geography that provides western narrative with its most compelling and durable image of India, which is, of course, the figure of India as a hollow, or a cave. It is the desire to know the hollow, but to leave defeated, that informs the dainty ironies of Forster's narrative, for the narrative mind can only empty its defeat upon the landscape, and depart from the area exhausted, but a little lighter. Since Forster, this model has been rehearsed repeatedly, but nowhere as effectively as in the ostensibly nonfictional text, V. S. Naipaul's *An Area of Darkness*. Both fictions share in that Western project which represents India as an empty site that is bounded only by an aura of irrationality. In examining the two narratives as a genealogical unit, I will attempt to chart the development of that amorphous idiom which begins in the novel an Englishman writes about India, but finally gains a nonfictional authority in the work of an Indian writer fully prepared to cite himself as a living emblem of India's inauthenticity.

In my reading, *A Passage to India* and *An Area of Darkness* are remarkably predisposed towards complete alignment. They are not only the two best British novels about India, but constitute parallel texts where the question posed by one is answered by the other. What can happen here? asks Forster: nothing, responds V. S. Naipaul, except history as the act of possible imagination, because there is only me. He thus proceeds to literalize Forster's image of disappointing emptiness by representing himself as the one self-conscious embodiment of India's massive failure to present a cohesive shape. Whereas this failure functions as the atmospherics of *A Passage to India*, in *An Area of Darkness* it becomes as palpable as the excrement that so appalls Naipaul that he must note and describe it each time it comes his way. To the imperial English mind, India can only be represented as a gesture of possible rape; to the post-colonial and equally English mind, India is nothing more than the imbecile act of self-exposure, whose outrage is too literal to allow for even the secrecy of shame.

That the Orient has traditionally been represented as a figure of seduction, duplicity—and, more darkly, rape—is a commonplace that is clearly established by European historical and travel narratives from the seventeenth century on. It takes Forster, however, to carry the rape image to its most finely wrought conclusion. While *A Passage to India* ostensibly centers on an hysteric who believes she has been raped, the course of the narrative suggests that the real outrage lies in the fact that this rude encounter has been withheld from her. India diffuses into emptiness before it completes the seduction it had promised, as though its own formlessness demands that it can be master of only an incomplete performance. Rape becomes, therefore, dangerously synonymous with sexual disappointment: that the novel is traversed by Western travelers invaded by sensations of impotence as long as they remain on Western territory is a crucial index of Forster's obsession with representing India as a figure of both an erotic yet sterile duplicity.

Forster's narrative is found, and founders on, the idiom of a god who neglects to come. In the key scene where the Hindu Godbole sings for the uncomprehending audience of Fielding's Muslim and British guests, he offers the following commentary:

> "It was a religious song. I placed myself in the position of a milkmaiden. I say to Shri Krishna, 'Come! come to me only.' The god refuses to come. I grow humble and say: 'Do not come to me only. Multiply yourself into a hundred Krishnas. . . . Come, come, come, come, come, come. He neglects to come.' "

Despite the parodic sentimentality of this version of Hinduism, the passage nonetheless provides Forster with a refrain that he uses to envelop all the inhabitants of India, where the god neglects to come. The structure of the novel images this neglect through its emblematic representation of empty institutions, or buildings that are somewhat wanton in their lack of habitation. *A Passage to India* makes neat architecture of this lack, in that the three sections of the book—"Mosque," "Caves," and "Temple"—function primarily as cavities to contain western perceptions of that which is missing from the East. The edifices thus constitute shells into which Forster can uncurl echoes of what first appears to be a humane compassion, but what gradually and more threateningly develops into an exquisite nostalgia for betrayal. While the novel attempts to delineate a Hindu "type" as opposed to a Muslim "type" in its portrayal of native characters like Godbole and Aziz, finally the Muslim merely represents a slightly obscene accessibility that is less than authentically Indian, while the Hindu becomes a little too Indian to be true, always teetering on the brink of transfiguration. Both Mosque and Temple, therefore, collaborate and collapse into the emptiness that is the Cave.

How does one traverse a landscape replete with images of Krishna, but where Krishna will not come? Forster's response, of course, is to construct a retreat through a dualistic vocabulary in which India is ultimately reprehensible because it denies the fixity of an object that the narrative subject can pursue and penetrate. Instead, like the self-dissipating echoes in the Marabar caves, it can only be approached as a sexuality that lacks a cleft, or a single certain entry of understanding. Throughout the novel, Forster manipulates the image of landscape as metaphoric of that possible fulfillment which is continually on the verge of emptying into disappointment. Finally, his only mode to chart the symbolic geography he names India is by means of locating a structure that perfectly resonates with its own absence. Here, he invites his readership to join him in the Marabar caves.

Forster approaches the caves with the polite bewilderment of an intelligent tourist guide who wishes to be respectful of an entity that is really not very interesting. The restraint with which the narrative seeks to image the cave's unbeauty is, however, its secret method of attack:

> The caves are readily described. A tunnel eight feet long, five feet high, three feet wide, leads to a circular chamber about twenty feet in diameter. This arrangement occurs again and again throughout the group of hills, and this is all, this is a Marabar Cave. Having seen one such cave, having seen two, having seen three, four, fourteen, twenty-four, the visitor returns to Chandrapore uncertain whether he has had an interesting experience or a dull one or any experience at all. He finds it difficult to discuss the caves, or to keep them apart in his mind. . . . Nothing, nothing attaches to them, and their reputation—for they have one — does not depend upon human speech.

The crevices that are India, in other words, are completely exposed to description, but are offensively impervious to interpretation, like the obscene echo that so torments Forster's female characters. To the western imagination, the horror of the caves is their lack of metaphoricity and their indifference to experiential time. That they could represent an historical autonomy can only be envisioned as a nightmare, or as a parodic pretension towards meaning. After having named the caves as areas of empty experience, the narrative proceeds to explore the hideous possibility that they may indeed possess strata of significance:

> But elsewhere, deeper in the granite, are there certain chambers that have no entrances? Chambers never unsealed since the arrival of the gods. Local report declares that these exceed in num-

ber those that can be visited, as the dead exceed the living—four
hundred of them, four thousand or million. Nothing is inside
them, they were sealed up before the creation of pestilence or
treasure; if mankind grew curious and excavated, nothing, nothing would be added to the sum of good or evil.

To entertain such a possibility, however, as Fielding attempts and fails to
entertain Indians and Europeans to tea, merely corroborates the narrative
fear that India is only real in prehistory, or when it arrives after the fact of
history. In relation to the existing authority of western narrative, India
represents the terrifying docility of Cordelia's nothing, and the further
obscenity of that word in the face of power, which knows that nothing can
come of nothing.

It is therefore a matter of some perplexity that most of Forster's readers
still see in *A Passage to India* a dated kindliness towards the "Indian question," or an imperial allegory in which an unattractive European female
falsely accuses an attractive Indian male of rape. In considering Adela
Quested, it is difficult to ignore the complicated defences that cause Forster
to represent her as a cipher almost as arid as the Marabar caves. For rather
than a woman abused or abusive, Adela essentially plays the part of a conduit
or a passageway for the aborted eroticism between the European Fielding
and the Indian Aziz. That, finally, is the substance of the novel: the narrative
is not brought to rest with the melodramatic rape trial and Adela's recan-
tation, but is impelled into a description of the Indian's ugly failure to
apprehend a European sensibility, and the seductive qualities of his con-
tinuing ignorance. Aziz's Muslim accessibility is made impenetrable by such
an ignorance, which allows the novel to conclude with the "half-kissing"
embrace of the two men who know that rape is unavailable, "not yet,"
"not here." The potential seduction of India is thus perpetuated by the
lovely, half-realized slave-boys of Forster's will to power; his revulsion
takes the darker shapes of the caves and the empty nothings of Adela
Quested's requesting womb.

Finally, what prevents the European and the Indian from completing
their embrace is the obliterating presence of the landscape. The European
wants the completion of his desire in the present moment, yet the narrative
gives the last word to the land's great power to deny and disappear:

But the horses didn't want it—they swerved apart; the earth
didn't want it . . . the temples, the tank, the jail, the palace, the
birds, the carrion, the Guest House . . . they didn't want it, they

said in their hundred voices, "No, not yet," and the sky said,
"No, not there."

With this concluding sentence, even the difference of India is subsumed
into a trope for a vacant and inexplicable rejection. It becomes instead an
unimaginable space which cannot be inhabited by the present tense, resisting
even the European attempt to coax it into metaphoricity.

Chronology

1879   Edward Morgan Forster born in London on January 1. His father, an architect of Anglo-Irish descent, dies the following year. His mother is descended from the Thornton family, of "Clapham Sect" fame.

1883–93   Forster lives in Hertfordshire at the home that will be the prototype of *Howards End*.

1887   Forster's favorite aunt, Marianne Thornton, dies, leaving him a legacy of £8,000.

1893   Forster's family moves to Tonbridge, where he attends Tonbridge School as a day boy.

1897   Enters King's College, Cambridge, where he studies Classics (B.A., 1900) and History (B.A., 1901; M.A., 1910). Among the teachers that influence Forster: Goldsworthy Lowes Dickinson, J. M. E. McTaggert, Roger Fry, and Nathaniel Wedd.

1901   Forster travels to Italy and Greece; lives in Italy until 1902, when he moves to Abinger Hammer, Surrey.

1903   Forster's first short story, "Albergo Empedocle," is published in *Temple Bar*. Several of his Cambridge friends, including Dickinson, G. M. Trevelyan, Wedd, and Edward Jenks, found the *Independent Review,* to which he will contribute.

1905   *Where Angels Fear to Tread* published.

1907   *The Longest Journey* published.

1908   *A Room with a View* published.

1910   *Howards End* published.

1911   *The Celestial Omnibus and Other Short Stories* published.

1912–13   Forster takes his first trip to India with Dickinson and R. C. Trevelyan. The visit, lasting from October until March, includes a stay with the Maharajah of Dewas Senior.

1914   Essays and reviews for *New Weekly*.

1915–19	Volunteer officer with the Red Cross in Alexandria, Egypt.
1919	Forster becomes literary editor of the *Daily Herald,* a Labour publication.
1921	Returns to India, as private secretary to the Maharajah of Dewas Senior. At the end of his stay he is presented with the Tukyjirao Gold Medal, the highest honor possible for a Westerner.
1922	*Alexandria: A History and a Guide* published.
1923	A collection of essays and sketches, *Pharos and Pharillon,* published.
1924	*A Passage to India* published. All the novels are reissued.
1925	Forster receives the Femina Vie Heureuse and James Tait Black Memorial Prizes for *A Passage to India.*
1927	*Aspects of the Novel,* a lecture series presented at Cambridge during this year, published. Forster is elected a Fellow of King's College.
1928	*The Eternal Moment and Other Stories* published.
1934	Forster's first biography, *Goldsworthy Lowes Dickinson,* is published. *The Abinger Pageant,* one of several dramatic efforts, is produced at Abinger Hammer. Forster becomes the first president of the National Council for Civil Liberties. He is elected again in 1942 and resigns in 1948.
1936	A collection of essays, *Abinger Harvest: A Miscellany,* published.
1939	*What I Believe* published.
1940	*Nordic Twilight* and *England's Pleasant Land, A Pageant Play* published.
1941	Forster delivers the Rede Lecture on Virginia Woolf.
1943	The first major critical work on Forster is published by Lionel Trilling (*E. M. Forster*), accompanied by the republication of all Forster's novels. This initiates a Forster revival in the United States.
1945	October–December, third visit to India, for a conference in Jaipur. After his mother's death, Forster accepts honorary fellowship at King's College, Cambridge, his chief residence for the rest of his life.
1947	At Harvard University symposium on music criticism, gives lecture "The Raison d'Etre of Criticism in the Arts." *Collected Tales* published in the United States.
1948	*Collected Short Stories* published in England.

1949   "Art for Art's Sake" given as lecture at the American Academy of Arts and Letters.

1951   *Two Cheers for Democracy,* a collection of essays, published. Honorary degree from Nottingham University. *Billy Budd,* an opera written in collaboration with Eric Crozier and Benjamin Britten, produced at Covent Garden.

1953   Awarded membership in the Order of Companions of Honor to the Queen by Elizabeth II. *The Hill of Devi,* a memoir of his first two India trips, is published.

1956   *Marianne Thornton,* a biography of Forster's aunt, published.

1961   Forster named Companion of Literature by the Royal Society of Literature.

1969   Forster awarded the Order of Merit.

1970   On June 7, Forster dies at the age of 91.

Contributors

HAROLD BLOOM, Sterling Professor of the Humanities at Yale University, is the author of *The Anxiety of Influence, Poetry and Repression,* and many other volumes of literary criticism. His forthcoming study, *Freud: Transference and Authority,* attempts a full-scale reading of all of Freud's major writings. A MacArthur Prize Fellow, he is general editor of five series of literary criticism published by Chelsea House.

LIONEL TRILLING, University Professor at Columbia University, was one of the most eminent critics in American literary history. His works include *The Liberal Imagination: Essays on Literature and Society, Beyond Culture: Essays on Literature and Learning,* and *Sincerity and Authenticity.*

MALCOLM BRADBURY, Fellow of the Royal Society of Literature, is Professor of American Studies at the University of East Anglia. His works include an edited volume, *E. M. Forster: A Collection of Critical Essays,* A Passage to India: *A Casebook,* and *The Social Context of Modern English Literature.*

K. NATWAR-SINGH has been in the Indian Foreign Service since 1953. He has written a number of books, including *E. M. Forster: A Tribute, The Legacy of Nehru,* and *Tales from Modern India.*

MICHAEL ORANGE is Lecturer in English at the University of Sydney.

BARBARA ROSECRANCE is Assistant Professor of English at Cornell University and has been an assistant editor of *Partisan Review.* She has written on Forster, early modern British literature, and the poetry and music of the Renaissance.

RUSTOM BHARUCHA teaches dramaturgy and criticism at the State University of New York at Stony Brook. He is now working on a collection of essays entitled *Double Exposure.*

SARA SULERI is Assistant Professor of English at Yale University. Her book in progress is on Wordsworth, Arnold, and Yeats.

Bibliography

Allen, Walter. *The English Novel*. New York: Dutton, 1955.

Ault, Peter. "Aspects of E. M. Forster." *Dublin Review* 219 (October 1946): 109–34.

Bedient, Calvin. *Architects of the Self: George Eliot, D. H. Lawrence, and E. M. Forster*. Berkeley and Los Angeles: University of California Press, 1972.

Beer, Gillian. "Negation in *A Passage to India*." *Essays in Criticism* 30, no. 2 (April 1980): 151–66.

Beer, J. B. *The Achievement of E. M. Forster*. New York: Barnes & Noble, 1962.

Beer, John, ed. A Passage to India: *Essays in Interpretation*. London: Macmillan, 1985.

Bell, Quentin. *Bloomsbury*. London: Weidenfeld & Nelson, 1968.

Bodenheimer, Rosemarie. "The Romantic Impasse in *A Passage to India*." *Criticism* 22, no. 1 (Winter 1980): 40–56.

Bowen, Elizabeth. "E. M. Forster." In *Collected Impressions*, 119–26. London: Longmans Green, 1950.

Bradbury, Malcolm, ed. *E. M. Forster:* A Passage to India. London: Macmillan, 1970.

Brower, Reuben Arthur. "The Twilight of the Double Vision: Symbol and Irony in *A Passage to India*." In *The Fields of Light*. New York: Oxford University Press, 1951.

Brown, E. K. *Rhythm in the Novel*. Toronto: University of Toronto Press, 1950.

Burke, Kenneth. "Social and Cosmic Mystery: *A Passage to India*." In *Language as Symbolic Action: Essays on Life, Literature, and Method*, 223–39. Berkeley and Los Angeles: University of California Press, 1968.

Burra, Peter. "The Novels of E. M. Forster." *Nineteenth Century and After* 116 (November 1935): 581–94.

Cammarota, Richard S. "Musical Analogy and Internal Design." *English Literature in Transition* 18, no. 1 (1975): 38–46.

Colmer, John. *E. M. Forster: The Personal Voice*. London and Boston: Routledge & Kegan Paul, 1975.

Crews, Frederick. *E. M. Forster: The Perils of Humanism*. Princeton: Princeton University Press, 1962.

Daleski, H. M. "Rhythmic and Symbolic Patterns in *A Passage to India*." In *Studies in English Language and Literature*, edited by Alice Shalvi and A. A. Mendilow. Jerusalem: Hebrew University, 1966.

Das, G. K., and John Beer, eds. *E. M. Forster: A Human Exploration (Centenary Essays)*. London: Macmillan, 1979.

Dowling, David. *Bloomsbury Aesthetics and the Novels of Forster and Woolf.* London: Macmillan, 1985.

Faulkner, Peter. *Humanism in the English Novel*. London: Elek/Pemberton, 1976.

Friend, Robert. "The Quest for Rondure: A Comparison of Two Passages to India." *The Hebrew University Studies in Literature* 1, no. 1 (Spring 1973): 76–85.

Furbank, P. N. *E. M. Forster: A Life*. 2 vols. London: Secker & Warburg, 1977.

Gardner, Philip, ed. *E. M. Forster: The Critical Heritage*. London and Boston: Routledge & Kegan Paul, 1973.

Gillie, Christopher. *A Preface to Forster.* London: Longman Group, 1983.

Gransden, K. W. *E. M. Forster*. Edinburgh and London: Oliver & Boyd, 1962.

Hardy, Barbara. *The Appropriate Form*. Evanston, Ill.: Northwestern University Press, 1971.

Herz, Judith Scherer, and Robert K. Martin, eds. *E. M. Forster: Centenary Revaluations*. Toronto: University of Toronto Press, 1982.

Johnstone, J. K. *The Bloomsbury Group: A Study of E. M. Forster, Lytton Strachey, Virginia Woolf, and Their Circle*. New York: Noonday Press, 1954.

Kermode, Frank. "The One Orderly Product (E. M. Forster)." In *Puzzles and Epiphanies: Essays and Reviews 1958–1961*. New York: Chilmark Press, 1962.

Langbaum, Robert. "A New Look at E. M. Forster." *Southern Review* 4 (Winter 1968): 33–49.

Leavis, F. R. "E. M. Forster." *Scrutiny* 7 (September 1938): 185–202.

Macaulay, Rose. *The Writings of E. M. Forster*. New York: Harcourt, Brace, 1938.

McConkey, James. *The Novels of E. M. Forster*. Ithaca: Cornell University Press, 1957.

McDowell, Frederick P. W. *E. M. Forster*. Revised edition. Boston: Twayne, 1982.

Meyers, Jeffrey. "The Politics of *Passage to India*." *Journal of Modern Literature* 1, no. 3 (March 1971): 329–38.

Natwar-Singh, K., ed. *E. M. Forster: A Tribute*. New York: Harcourt, Brace & World, 1964.

Pradhan, S. V. "*A Passage to India*: Realism versus Symbolism, A Marxist Analysis." *Dalhousie Review* 60, no. 2 (Summer 1980): 300–317.

Richards, I. A. "A Passage to Forster." *Forum* 78 (December 1927): 914–29.

Rutherford, Andrew, ed. *Twentieth-Century Interpretations of* A Passage to India. Englewood Cliffs, N.J.: Prentice-Hall, 1970.

Schwarz, Daniel R. "The Originality of E. M. Forster." *Modern Fiction Studies* 29, no. 4 (Winter 1983): 623–41.

Shahane, V. A., ed. *Perspectives on E. M. Forster's* A Passage to India: *A Collection of Critical Essays*. New York: Barnes & Noble, 1968.

Shusterman, David. *The Quest for Certitude in E. M. Forster's Fiction*. Bloomington: Indiana University Press, 1965.

Spender, Stephen. "Personal Relations and Public Powers." In *The Creative Element: A Study of Vision, Despair, and Orthodoxy among Some Modern Writers*. London: Hamish Hamilton, 1953.

Stallybrass, Oliver, ed. *Aspects of E. M. Forster: Essays and Recollections Written for*

His Ninetieth Birthday, January 1, 1969. New York: Harcourt, Brace & World, 1969.

Stone, Wilfred. *The Cave and the Mountain: A Study of E. M. Forster.* Stanford, Calif.: Stanford University Press, 1966.

Summers, Claude J. *E. M. Forster.* New York: Frederick Ungar, 1983.

Thomson, George H. *The Fiction of E. M. Forster.* Detroit: Wayne State University Press, 1967.

Thumboo, Edwin. "E. M. Forster's *A Passage to India:* From Caves to Court." *Southern Review* 10, no. 4 (December 1978): 386–404.

Turk, Jo M. "The Evolution of E. M. Forster's Narrator." *Studies in the Novel* 5, no. 4 (Winter 1973): 428–39.

Warren, Austin. "The Novels of E. M. Forster." In *Rage for Order,* 119–41. Chicago: University of Chicago Press, 1948.

Wilde, Alan. *Art and Order: A Study of E. M. Forster.* New York: New York University Press, 1964.

———. "Depths and Surfaces: Dimensions of Forsterian Irony." *English Literature in Transition* 16, no. 4 (1973): 257–73.

Acknowledgments

"*A Passage to India*" by Lionel Trilling from *E. M. Forster: A Study by Lionel Trilling* by Lionel Trilling, © 1944 by Lionel Trilling. Reprinted by permission of New Directions Publishing Co. and Laurence Pollinger Ltd.

"Two Passages to India: Forster as Victorian and Modern" by Malcolm Bradbury from *Aspects of E. M. Forster,* edited by Oliver Stallybrass, © 1969 by Edward Arnold Publishers Ltd. Reprinted by permission.

"Only Connect . . . : Forster and India" by K. Natwar-Singh from *Aspects of E. M. Forster,* edited by Oliver Stallybrass, © 1969 by Edward Arnold Publishers Ltd. Reprinted by permission.

"Language and Silence in *A Passage to India*" by Michael Orange from *E. M. Forster: A Human Exploration: Centenary Essays,* edited by G. K. Das and John Beer, © 1979 by Michael Orange. Reprinted by permission of the Macmillan Press Ltd. and Rowan & Littlefield, Totowa, NJ.

"*A Passage to India:* Forster's Narrative Vision" (originally entitled "A Passage to India") by Barbara Rosecrance, © 1982 by Cornell University Press. Reprinted by permission of the publisher.

"Forster's Friends" by Rustom Bharucha from *Raritan: A Quarterly Review* 5, no. 4 (Spring 1986), © 1986 by *Raritan,* 165 College Avenue, New Brunswick, NJ. Reprinted by permission.

"The Geography of *A Passage to India*" by Sara Suleri, © 1987 Sara Suleri. Printed by permission.

Index

Abbott, Caroline *(Howards End)*, 24
Adl, Mohammed-el, 97–99
Alexandria: A History and a Guide, 12; religion in, 5–7
Ali, Ahmed, 55
Ali, Mahmound, 86
Ali, Mohammed, 96
Ali, Shaukat, 96
Allen, Walter, 33
Ambassadors, The (James), 86
Anand, Mulk Raj, 55
Anglo-Indians: arrogance of, 19–20, 50–51, 52–53; Forster's characterization of, 17, 38, 85, 101–2; and Kipling, 46; and reaction to *A Passage to India*, 49
Archer, Isabel *(Portrait of a Lady)*, 2
Area of Darkness, An (Naipaul), 109
Arnold, Matthew, 32
Arnold, William Delafield, 26
Austen, Jane, 33
Autobiography (Nehru), 52–53
Aziz: accessibility of, 110, 112; appeal to God of, 77–78; and denial of meaning, 37; and echo theme, 23; estrangement from Fielding of, 10, 20, 21, 26, 61, 86; exclusion from India of, 71, 104; expression of masculinity of, 97; and

Fielding, 79, 96, 103, 112; Forster's sympathy with, 102; as member of subject race, 18, 21; and Mrs. Moore, 19, 25; as Muslim, 54, 104, 110; nationalism of, 96–97; and Ralph Moore, 26, 79, 103; sentimentality of, 70, 84; silences of, 67, 68; weaknesses of, 1–2, 18, 76; and world of the heart, 39

Bahadur, Nawab, 23, 61, 62, 85
Bhagavad-Gita, 54–55
British-Indian relations: and cultural differences, 20, 60–61; and ethos of masculinity, 95–96; Forster's position on, 12, 52, 112; and Hindu vision of emptiness, 26; irony of, 39; and language, 60; and male bonding, 96; and sexuality, 94–95; and symbolic geography, 112–13; "undeveloped heart" as problem in, 20, 46
Brown, E. K., 35
Butler, Samuel, 12, 33

Campbell, Joseph, 60
Carella, Gino (Howards End), 21
Christianity: vs. Hinduism, 9; inadequacy of, 22, 25, 26, 70

127